RYDE
RAIL

RYDE
RAIL

A History of Tube Trains
on the **Isle of Wight**

Richard C Long

crecy.co.uk

For Mum and Dad

First published in 2019 by Crécy Publishing

Printed in Turkey by Olas Solutions

ISBN 978 191080 9570

www.crecy.co.uk

Crécy Publishing Limited
1a Ringway Trading Estate, Shadowmoss Road,
Manchester M22 5LH
www.crecy.co.uk

Front cover: Network SouthEast-liveried Standard Stock unit No 485041 climbs the 1 in 80 gradient between Sandown and Lake in the hot afternoon sun of 19 July 1989. *Martyn Hilbert*

Back cover inset clockwise from top:
Departing north from Smallbrook Junction on 27 June 2001, unit No 009 is followed by No 002, which proudly displays its 'Raptor' name – quite possibly the only unit to regularly carry its allocated dinosaur name. *Andy Sansome*

Four months after being re-released into traffic, an immaculate London Transport-liveried No 007 stands at Shanklin on 25 May 2003. *Nick Doolan collection*

One day after its arrival at Fishbourne, car No S22S is carefully manoeuvred into the yard at Ryde St John's Road on 22 December 1966. *J. Mackett, IWSR Archive*

VEC unit No 045 is seen here on test at Weybridge on the mainland on 28 March 1967 – more than a week after electric services had launched on the Isle of Wight. *Colour-Rail.com*

Back cover main:
An unidentified 1938 Stock unit traverses Ryde Pier in the subtropical climate of August 2018. Ryde Pier Head is out-of-shot to the right and Ryde Esplanade to the left. *Shariff Moossun, Aerialview.org.uk*

Half title: 3-TIS unit No 032 is stabled in the siding at the north end of Ryde St John's Road station on 9 July 1985. *Gordon Edgar*

Frontispiece: 1938 Stock unit No 004 passes Yarbridge, half a mile south of Brading, forming the 15.49 Ryde Pier Head to Shanklin working on 6 July 2017. *Martyn Hilbert*

Contents

Acknowledgements 6

1   Closure or Modernisation? 7

2   Electrification 15

3   The End of the Pier Tram 30

4   From British Rail to Ryde Rail 43

5   The Diesel Shunters 60

6   The Network SouthEast Years 70

7   Privatisation 88

8   The Final Years of Tube Train Operation? 101

Appendix The Class 503 Proposal 124

Notes 134

Bibliography 140

Index 141

Acknowledgements

As ever I should like to express my thanks to all those who have assisted or supported me in the writing of this volume. I'm particularly grateful to all of the photographers named throughout the book, without whom it would not have been possible in its current form. I'd also like to record my gratitude, in no particular order, to Roger Silsbury, Roger MacDonald, Nigel Brodrick, Mark Brinton, Nick Brown, Derek Gawn and Daniel Wright for all their help and assistance in various ways. I'd like to thank anyone with whom I've discussed anything in online forums, including the members of the various Isle of Wight railway Facebook groups, which might have had any bearing on anything mentioned in the text. I'm grateful to my father for letting me store my old copies of *Rail* and *Motive Power Monthly* in his loft for the past 25 years, and to my brother for driving said magazines up to London when I needed them for research. And finally thanks are due to the staff at Crécy Publishing, and in particular to Kevin Robertson for letting me persuade him that this might actually be a good idea for a book.

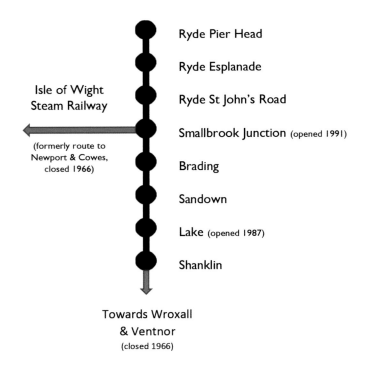

Ryde Pier Head

Ryde Esplanade

Ryde St John's Road

Isle of Wight Steam Railway

(formerly route to Newport & Cowes, closed 1966)

Smallbrook Junction (opened 1991)

Brading

Sandown

Lake (opened 1987)

Shanklin

Towards Wroxall & Ventnor (closed 1966)

Closure or Modernisation?

The Beeching Report

On 20 November 1953 a conference was held in Newport, the Isle of Wight's county town, to consider the future of the Island's transport network after the recent closure of three of its railway lines: the Ventnor West branch in 1952 and the Freshwater and Bembridge branches in 1953. The outcome of this gathering was summed up by the local newspaper, the *Isle of Wight County Press*, with the headline: 'Island Railways: Probable Life of Ten Years'.[1] Nine and a half years later this prediction seemed about to come true when *The Reshaping of British Railways* (better known as the 'Beeching Report') was published.

'The Isle of Wight will have no trains left,' reported *The Times* on 28 March 1963.[2] Yet despite this, and similar headlines in the *County Press*, British Railways was not actually proposing to pull out of the Island altogether. Of the three Ryde stations, only Ryde St John's Road appeared under the heading 'Passenger Stations and Halts to be Closed' in Beeching's report. Having recently decided to

embark upon a quarter-of-a-million-pound refurbishment of Ryde Pier, BR was not now proposing to close the stations at Ryde Pier Head or Ryde Esplanade. Within days of the Beeching Report being published it was revealed that, but for the intervention of the Island's MP and County Council the previous year, these repairs would never have been agreed and the entire network might have been abandoned by the end of 1963.[3]

Beeching anticipated

Dr Beeching's proposals were not unanticipated. The Isle of Wight had lost around half of its 55½-mile railway network in the 1950s, with the closures of 1952-53 followed by the loss of the Newport-Sandown line in 1956. Ever since then the closure of the rest of the system had been prophesied, and the appointment of Dr Richard Beeching as Chairman of the British Railways Board in June 1961, with a remit of making the railways profitable, did little to calm fears. In October of that year Mary Lovegrove of Niton wrote to the

How things used to be: holidaymakers prepare to board their train at Ryde Pier Head while Adams 'O2' tank engine No W24 *Calbourne* stands at the buffer stops of Platform 1. The sign at the entrance to the platform lists all stations to Ventnor, while that at the entrance to Platform 2 displays all stations to Cowes; between them these two routes comprised the entire Isle of Wight railway network in the years 1956-66.
K. C. H. Fairey, Colour-Rail.com

County Press to say: 'Dr Beeching's next bright idea will probably be to close the Ryde-Ventnor line as "uneconomic".'[4] Ms Lovegrove was not alone in her concerns and such comments would become common in the letters pages of the County Press in the months leading up to the publication of the 1963 Beeching Report. But how could such a fate be avoided? Some correspondents favoured capitalising on the age of the Island's by now ancient rolling stock and following in the footsteps of the UK's first standard-gauge heritage railway:

> 'I would refer readers to the case of the Bluebell Railway in Sussex, which has thrived for two years on the fact that the stock is old. It is a working museum of railway history. In a different way the Island is like the Bluebell line…
>
> Would the expense of bringing more engines to the Island be worth while when the present engines, 70 years old or not, continue to function perfectly well?'[5]

Sadly, however, the reality was that the Victorian engines were reaching the end of their working lives. 'They cannot be expected to run indefinitely,' noted another reader, who reported that many had cracked frames.[6] Overall the vast majority of Islanders, or at least those who wrote to the County Press, seemed to be in agreement that their railways were a vital transport network, not a heritage attraction, and that modernisation was the only way forward. Just weeks before the publication of the Beeching Report a Mr Norris of Ryde predicted that 'the lines upon which the axe will fall are obviously already picked – they are the lines upon which no modernisation attempt has been made.'[7] But even if the axe were to be avoided, what form should this modernisation take and where might new rolling stock come from?

The Bennie Airspeed Railway

Perhaps the most remarkable proposal to replace the Isle of Wight's ageing rolling stock had come as long ago as 1953 when, with closures already under way, the inventor George Bennie had proposed taking over the entire Island network and converting it to a 'Bennie Airspeed Railway'. Essentially a cross between a monorail and a propeller-driven aircraft, Bennie's only working prototype had been constructed in Scotland in 1929-30, and his Isle of Wight proposal seems to have been largely forgotten by history. According to the County Press at the time, the £4 million scheme had 'the necessary financial backing and may be given support by the County Council when an approach is made to the Government for permission to provide an alternative means of transport.' A circular route was projected that would largely incorporate the existing routes together with a new direct Cowes to Ryde link. 'Although speeds of 200 miles an hour are possible, about 125 miles an hour would be the fastest on the Island.'[8] Bennie's proposal was short-lived, being rejected by the Council

once it was determined that, even at a rate of one passenger car per minute, the scheme would be unable to handle the Island's peak loads. Moreover, 'The cars were also too high to go through tunnels … a factor which the promoters did not seem to have considered.'[9]

The issue that Bennie seems to have overlooked was the fact that, being too large to use the tunnel, his monorail would have to go over St Boniface Down in order to reach Ventnor. This was not the last time that tunnels, or at least loading gauge issues, would play a part in determining the future of the Island's railways.

Replacement steam locomotives?

In complete contrast to George Bennie's futuristic proposal, the first serious consideration given by British Railways towards replacing the Isle of Wight's trains was to provide more second-hand steam locomotives, with Eastleigh Works drawing up plans in 1960 to convert members of the BR Standard Class 2 tanks to fit the Island's loading gauge. Having been built as recently as the mid-1950s, these would have been among the most modern stock ever to have operated on the Isle of Wight (and considerably newer than the tube trains serving the Island today). However, this would have only been a partial solution to the Island's rolling stock issues as the pre-Grouping wooden-bodied carriages were also approaching the end of their usage. With the Standard tanks in need of overhaul and closure of the network looking increasingly likely, the idea was quietly shelved. (This might-have-been scenario can be experienced on today's Isle of Wight Steam Railway, where two members of the similar Ivatt Class 2 tanks are now in regular service.)

Modern traction?

Contrary to what we might expect today, in the 1960s rail travellers were not overly nostalgic for the days of steam and favoured instead an altogether more modern form of transport. 'The time has come for the steam engines to be replaced by diesel units'[10]; 'an efficient clean diesel service would no doubt attract many back to this form of transport.'[11] One regular correspondent to the County Press on the subject was in no doubt as to exactly what sort of diesel units should be provided: 'not the boneshakers used by the Southern Region in Southern Hampshire, but the units used widely in the Midlands, West Country, East Anglia and the North… Anyone who has travelled in the front of one of these units will know, too, just how attractive a journey just behind the driver can be with a clear view of the line ahead.' Could these units be the saviour of the Island's railways? 'On many routes where they are used they have succeeded in increasing the number of travellers by anything up to 300 per cent.'[12] If true, this figure had obviously not been seen by another reader who had been sure that units 'must now be available from other districts whose branches have been closed.'[13] L. A. Jackson of Surrey had an alternative suggestion: 'What is required in the Island is a light electric railway like the London tubes…'[14]

'O2' Class No W20 *Shanklin* arrives at Ryde Pier Head in July 1964. In the early 1960s many Islanders were decidedly unromantic about their elderly steam engines, believing instead that 'an efficient clean diesel service' would save their railways from closure. *Ron Fisher*

Electrification?

In January 1962 a meeting of Cowes Council heard that 'Recently electric trains had been introduced for the first time in Scotland and there the number of passengers carried, and receipts, had increased by two-and-a-half times.' A dismissive written reply had been received from the General Manager of British Railways' Southern Region, noting that the electrification in question had taken place in Glasgow: 'It will be realised that … this increase resulted from a very different state of business and residential circumstances from those which apply on the Island.'[15]

Was electrification an option? Surprisingly it had been considered as far back as the early 20th century ('the Council conditionally agreed to give any such scheme its hearty approval,' noted the *County Press* in March 1907[16]). In the wake of the Beeching Report the possibility of conversion to light rail 'if the railway was taken over by the County Council or private enterprise' was also floated by the Island's Conservative MP, Alderman Mark Woodnutt, only to be firmly rebutted by a local union official who advised him: 'Quite frankly I cannot see any prospect at all of a railway being run as a tramway, or even by private enterprise on the present basis.'[17] Both light rail and local authority control would be suggested again as possibilities in the 21st century.

In any case, any question of modernisation, diesel, electric or otherwise, was surely academic after the publication of Beeching's 1963 report – or was it?

Opposition to Beeching

The publication of the Beeching Report in March 1963 caused a great deal of outcry on the Isle of Wight, not least because of the potential damage to the annual holiday traffic on which so much of the Island's economy depended. Individual Islanders, local councils, the County Council, trade unions, various hotel and business associations; all were united in their opposition to the proposals. Alderman Woodnutt MP, finding himself at odds with his own government, threatened to resign the party whip if closures went ahead.

The Island's situation was unique, or at least so its inhabitants believed. According to British Railways' own figures, the Island's railways 'carried more than 5,000 passengers a week'[18] but the truth was that most of these passengers were holidaymakers carried during the course of a few short weeks over the summer, with up to 3,000 passengers *an hour* estimated to arrive by boat at Ryde Pier Head on summer Saturdays. The majority of these continued their journey by rail south of Ryde towards the holiday resorts of Sandown, Shanklin and Ventnor. The road network was already stretched, with police figures showing 33,000 cars per day, or around 75 vehicles a mile, on the roads during the summer season – 'the highest density in the country,' according to the Police Chief Superintendent.[19] The *County Press* spoke for most Islanders when it said:

An unidentified 'O2' Class tank engine takes water at Newport at the head of a train to Ryde Pier Head in July 1964. Newport is the Isle of Wight's county town but, with the bulk of the tourist traffic concentrated on the Ryde to Ventnor line, that in itself would not be enough to save the Newport line from closure. *Ron Fisher*

county town of Newport and also generated the bulk of the freight traffic – which arrived on the Island via Medina Wharf. Nonetheless, freight flows were no longer as important as they had once been and none of this seemed enough to warrant a spirited defence of the Cowes route.

Shortly after the publication of the Beeching Report Alderman Woodnutt MP advised Ventnor Conservatives: 'He thought alternative transport could be provided for the Ryde-Newport-Cowes line and if it was possible to do so for that line then they must agree, but he was quite dogmatic about the line to Ventnor.'[22] Two months later he told the TUC that he would be willing to 'do a deal' over the Cowes line provided the Ryde-Ventnor line could be kept open.[23] But would British Railways, or the Government, be willing to do a deal?

All change at Ryde?

Following the publication of the Beeching Report a British Railways official met with representatives from the Isle of Wight authorities and local business organisations in Newport on 27 May 1963 to explain BR's plans in detail. Mr F. P. B. Taylor, Line Manager of the South Western Division, reported that the intention was to convert the existing railway pier for an enhanced tramway operation between Pier Head and Esplanade (this was apparently in addition to the existing Ryde Pier Tram, which was also owned and operated by BR). On the Esplanade itself, the land released by the closure of the railway would then be used as a bus station for the services that would carry passengers onward to their destinations. One alternative option, noted the *County Press*, had already been ruled out: 'They had considered … taking the buses to the pierhead, but had concluded that this would be expensive and not entirely practicable.' The line manager was evidently not in a mood for compromise; when asked how families with prams were expected to travel on buses, 'Mr Taylor replied that the pram could be sent luggage in advance through the railways!'[24]

BR may have ruled out a bus station at the pier head, but that was exactly what a special committee of Ryde Town Council was recommending two months later in August 1963, having concluded that 'under no circumstances would they be in favour of the establishment of a bus or coach station on Ryde Esplanade.' One other option was suggested, reported the *County Press*:

'Trains are able to cope, but … it is obvious that we have neither the number of buses (each carrying about 60 passengers plus their luggage) nor the roads capable of carrying such traffic. Much of the rural charm of the Island would be destroyed if such facilities did exist.'[20]

(Needless to say, Southern Vectis, the local bus company, which stood to gain most from any railway closures, did not share this widely held view that it would be unable to cope with the increased traffic.)

Farewell to Cowes?

On publication of the Beeching Report it quickly became apparent that many of those leading the anti-closure campaign were setting their sights firmly on the goal of saving the Ryde-Ventnor line. 'If we are to retain our holiday industry it is essential that at least the coastal line is retained,' wrote the *County Press*.[21] The 'coastal line' referred to was that linking Ryde with the resorts of Sandown, Shanklin and Ventnor on the eastern coast, and it was this line that carried the bulk of the passenger traffic – around 2½ million passengers versus a mere 500,000 on the Ryde-Cowes line. The Cowes line did pass through the

'The second alternative, if the pier scheme should prove impracticable, is the conversion of Ryde St John's railway station into a bus or coach station, with a rail service to the pier head on the London Underground pattern.'[25]

By January 1964 the town council's suggestion was starting to look uncannily prophetic when the *County Press* received details of a BR staff consultation document:

'It is proposed to run a shuttle service between Ryde Pier Head and a rail/bus transfer point in Ryde. The shuttle service will be operated over the existing railway lines, probably with redundant London Transport Board stock…

The chief civil engineer has confirmed that the London Transport Board's tube stock can be operated between Ryde Pier, the Esplanade or Ryde St John's, subject to certain alterations, including platforms.'[26]

The document noted that 'if necessary' the tube trains could be converted for diesel operation.

Why tube trains?

Why was British Railways considering second-hand tube trains for the Isle of Wight? If any services were to be retained south of Ryde Esplanade they would have to contend with the constraints of the Island's restricted loading gauge and in particular the tunnel under Ryde, which had a clearance 10 inches lower than that of the mainland railways. The possibility of building new stock was out of the question on economic grounds (as it had been for a very long time – the Ryde to Ventnor line, the most prosperous on the Island, had received no new-build stock since the 19th century), and in 1963 a BR spokesperson had stated that 'There was now no rolling stock elsewhere suitable to be transferred to the Island.' That there was no suitable rolling stock elsewhere might have been true of the BR network but, as it turned out, London Transport had a ready supply of life-expired trains that were well within gauge for the Isle of Wight.

At least one *Railway Magazine* reader thought the option of converting tube trains to diesel operation was unnecessary:

'…providing the electrical equipment on the trains is available and in good order, the simplest thing is to make the island railways electric by laying second-hand conductor rails and installing the few rectifier substations which would be necessary… I think that the public would appreciate electric trains with their good windows, speed and greater comfort more than the present old carriages, and use them for journeys other than merely getting to and from the ferries.'[27]

'O2' Class No W28 *Ashey* is at Ventnor in July 1964 having just arrived from Ryde, and is running round its carriages, on the right, prior to forming the next northbound departure. In April 1963 the Island's MP stated that he was 'quite dogmatic about [saving] the line to Ventnor.' *Ron Fisher*

Closure notice

The question of where in Ryde to provide a bus interchange was still undecided by BR when in February 1964 it published an official notice in the *County Press* of its intention to withdraw 'all existing railway passenger services' on the Island:

'It is proposed to operate a shuttle service on the Railway between Ryde (Pier Head) and a rail/bus interchange point at Ryde to be agreed with the Isle of Wight County Council or, in default of agreement, as determined by the Minister.'[28]

According to the terms of the notice, existing services to Ventnor and Cowes were to be discontinued on 12 October that year, unless any objections were lodged with the South Eastern Area Transport Users' Consultative Committee (TUCC). The County Council was quick to respond, and elsewhere on the same page of the newspaper it was reported that the closure date had already been postponed following its objection to the TUCC. A public hearing would now have to be held at which any objections would be heard, after which the TUCC would report back to the Minister of Transport if it considered that any unnecessary hardship would be caused by the closure of the lines.

TUCC hearing

The three-day public hearing into the proposed closure of the Island's railways began at the County Hall, Newport, on 10 June 1964. From the outset it was clear that the TUCC was broadly sympathetic to the Islanders' case: 'We are satisfied … that there is hardship. Our duty is to try and quantify that hardship.' Representing the many objectors, Mr L. H. Baines, Clerk of the Isle of Wight County Council, presented a strong argument: 'It is difficult to imagine a case which would inflict greater hardship on the community… There is no doubt that this proposal would disrupt the economics of the Island for years to come.' Figures were presented showing that, owing to the limited capacity of the car ferries then in operation, most tourists had no choice but to leave their vehicles at home and travel around the Island by public transport. Almost half of the Island's horticultural crops were consumed by visitors, meaning that 'many would immediately go out of business' if tourist numbers dropped. Uniquely among English and Welsh counties, the Island had no trunk roads, meaning that ratepayers would bear at least 25% of the cost of the road improvements required if the railways were to cease – and these improvement works would take five to ten years to plan and implement. Evidence from a computer simulation ('a revolutionary form of evidence' noted the *County Press*) was produced to show that, among other things, there would be an extra 770 bus journeys squeezed through the narrow streets of Brading during a 16-hour day in the tourist season. Representing the British Railways Board, Mr F. P. B. Taylor was not impressed with this new technology; computers 'were insensible to personal feelings or to public behaviour.'

After lunch on the second day of the enquiry, before Mr Taylor had even given his evidence, the TUCC made a surprise unanimous announcement:

'Subject, obviously, to anything that the railways may have to say … in so far as the Ryde-Ventnor line is concerned prima facia case of severe hardship has been made out to the satisfaction of the committee.'

The committee was not unanimous in its opinion of the likely hardship to be caused by the closure of the Ryde-Cowes line, about which it felt it had heard very little.

Faced with the thankless task of presenting the case for closure to a committee that had already decided against it, Mr Taylor nonetheless attempted to argue that 'severe hardship' was already experienced by many commuters in the London area and defended the proposed bus terminal on Ryde Esplanade on the grounds that it would be larger, and therefore better able to cope, than the bus terminal outside London Victoria station! Noting the uncertainty regarding the Cowes line he argued that its passengers would be better suited by a bus service, and for the first time the possibility of retaining services as far south as Shanklin, but not Ventnor, was raised. In concluding his case he noted:

'If the railways were reprieved, whether in whole or in part, the board would soon have to face heavy capital expenditure. They had already had to spend more on the pier than was deemed necessary and more work was indicated… The rolling stock on the Island could not last much longer.'

The need to replace the rolling stock was one area on which Mr Baines and Mr Taylor were in agreement – Mr Baines: 'I do not believe there is anyone in the room who thinks that the present rolling stock can last for another 10 years'.[29]

The enquiry obviously left British Railways in a bit of a quandary. It now seemed likely that the TUCC would advise the Transport Minister, Ernest Marples (the very Minister that had commissioned the Beeching Report), that part or all of the existing Isle of Wight network south of Ryde should be saved. Would the Minister agree and could BR make any plans for the future until it knew how large the network would be?

In August 1964 BR acquired its first twelve tube carriages, which were delivered to Wimbledon depot, for potential use on the Isle of Wight. According to the *County Press*, these amounted to 'two trains' that 'would be available for a service between Ryde Pier Head and Ryde St John's Road station if Mr Marples decided to close the Island's remaining railway lines.' Bought at scrap prices, 'the trains would be there if needed. If not they could be re-sold.'[30]

Decision awaited

The originally planned closure date had been October 1964, but it was only early in that month that the TUCC

Ryde's railway pier was substantially rebuilt over several successive winters in the years leading up to electrification. This photo from circa 1965, showing a Grafton steam crane being used to construct new steel framework at the mouth of Ryde Pier Head station, indicates the extent of reconstruction undertaken. *J. Mackett, IWSR Archive*

finally submitted its report to the Minister of Transport. At this time the Minister was still Ernest Marples, but by the end of the month a General Election had taken place and a new Government was in power. If nothing else, this made things politically easier for the Isle of Wight's Conservative MP, Mark Woodnutt, who had retained his seat (no doubt in part because of his determined opposition to the closures). Up until now Alderman Woodnutt had been opposing his own government; if any closures went ahead now, the blame would fall upon the new Labour Minister of Transport, Tom Fraser.

By the end of the year a decision seemed as far away as ever, with Alderman Woodnutt expressing his frustrations in December: 'He had no more success with Mr Marples than he was having with the new Minister.'[31] The precise nature of the TUCC's recommendations were unknown; in October the Railway Invigoration Society had been told that 'Consultative Committee's reports on these matters are considered to be confidential'[32]. Tube historian Brian Hardy reports that by this time BR was already working on the assumption that the Ryde-Shanklin section was to be retained.[33]

The Minister's decision

It was more than a year after the TUCC hearing that a decision was finally reached, with *The Times* reporting on 29 July 1965 that 'the Minister of Transport has refused his consent to the withdrawal of passenger services between Ryde (Pier Head) and Shanklin, Isle of Wight.'[34] The remaining lines to Cowes and Ventnor were to close, while money was to be spent on modernising the Ryde-Shanklin route. It goes without saying that this was something of a compromise solution, being more than BR had originally wanted to keep open, but less than local campaigners had been asking for.

The *County Press* had further details, indicating that the partial reprieve had been granted not for the benefit of the local population but only for the sake of 'the large number of people travelling to and from the Island for holidays in summer'. Apparently the TUCC had advised that 'the retention of passenger services on the Ryde-Shanklin section would alleviate most of the hardship which the closure proposal would cause.' For the Island's MP, this was a partial victory; the 'main objective' had been achieved, but it was 'clearly nonsense' to close the Shanklin-Ventnor section. Criticising the Labour Party for 'broken election promises' (the local candidate had promised that a vote for Labour would 'save the Island's railways from Tory massacre'), Alderman Woodnutt's thoughts now turned to the nature of the proposed modernisation:

'The Member pointed out that the letter to the Railway Board does not state what sort of modernisation the Minister has in mind. Ald. Woodnutt was hoping that the minister does not merely intend to replace 1876 locomotives with steam engines built in 1914!'[35]

The MP's statement that the existing locomotives were as old as 1876 was out by about 15 years (perhaps he was recalling the Stroudley 'Terriers' that had once worked on the Island?) and his fear that more second-hand steam locomotives might be on their way proved to be very wide of the mark. One year later, while launching the first British Rail hovercraft service to the Isle of Wight, BR's Chairman would also welcome the fact that 'the tradition of maintaining public transport on the Island by the railway business will be continued in a modern form'.[36] What would this mean in practice?

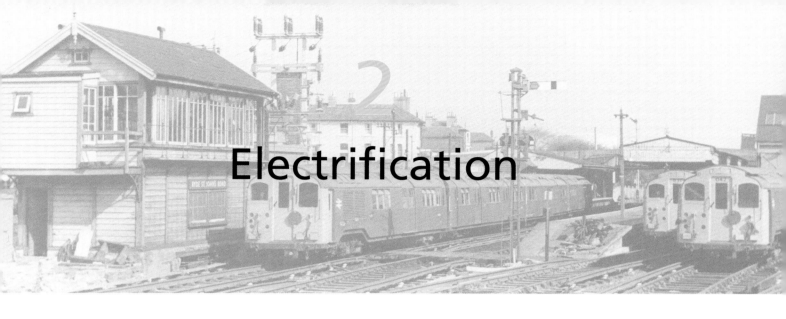

Electrification

At first glance, little would appear to have changed to returning holidaymakers arriving off the ferry at Ryde Pier Head in the summer of 1966. The familiar beat of a Westinghouse pump would still have been audible as an elderly Adams 'O2' tank waited at the head of a rake of wooden-bodied compartment coaches with the next southbound departure. On closer examination, however, the tourists would find their choice of destination severely curtailed, with Cowes, Newport, Wroxall and Ventnor all among the stations now absent from the Isle of Wight's railway map. By the summer of 1967 much more would have changed.

Closures

Having received ministerial approval in July 1965, it was not until January 1966 that the newly rebranded 'British Rail' announced the closure dates for the Ryde-Cowes and Shanklin-Ventnor lines. This time there would be no reprieve, and the closures went ahead as planned. Passenger traffic between Ryde and Cowes ceased on 21 February 1966, with the end of goods traffic in May marking the official end of 104 years of service for the former Cowes & Newport Railway, the Isle of Wight's earliest railway line. (In fact, the line would continue to see engineering trains until October, since conductor rails for the forthcoming electrification scheme were delivered via Medina Wharf.) The Shanklin-Ventnor line closed to all traffic from 18 April 1966, just months short of its centenary.

One week before the closure dates were revealed, BR had announced the first details of its plans for modernising the remaining Ryde-Shanklin line. Authority to electrify the railway had been granted and the entire line would be closed during the winter of 1966-67 while the work was undertaken. Speaking to the *County Press*, Mr D. V. Ellison, the Southern Region's Planning Manager, said, 'By the summer [of 1967] we ought to be raring to go'.[37]

Modernisation plans

The decision to electrify the Ryde-Shanklin line had been taken during 1965. BR had been stockpiling redundant tube cars for possible Isle of Wight use since 1964, and making use of the cars' existing electric motors was now considered cheaper than converting them for diesel operation.

The earlier diesel proposals might have borne some fruit elsewhere; the design of BR's Class 73 electro-diesel locomotives is sometimes reported as having been developed from abandoned plans for an Isle of Wight motorised luggage van.[38] Whatever the truth of this, it should be pointed out that the Class 73s as built were actually constructed to fit the formerly restrictive loading gauge of the Hastings line; they were not specifically designed to fit through Ryde Tunnel.

The decision to electrify using the third-rail system (albeit possibly at a lower voltage than the 750V DC used elsewhere on the Southern[39]), might have seemed obvious, but it did raise some eyebrows. The Southern Region and its predecessor, the Southern Railway, had been extending their electric network for decades, but since the Island's railway was completely isolated from the rest of the SR there was no obvious need for any operational compatibility with lines north of the Solent. Faced with a protest group's claims that overhead electrification would be cheaper, a British Rail spokesman responded, 'The old Southern Railway ran the two systems side-by-side and proved the third-rail system is best.'[40] In itself this statement is a little suspect since the SR's own experience of running the two systems side by side had been in the 1920s, while more recently, on a national level at least, BR had clearly decided that AC overhead electrification was the way forward. A more likely explanation was that overhead wires would have been incompatible both with clearance levels in Ryde Tunnel and with the tube stock that BR had already acquired. Was third-rail the only option? Presumably it was the cheapest, but it should be noted that the tube cars, built for operation on London Transport's fourth-rail network, now had to be converted for third-rail operation. One wonders if the alternative of installing fourth-rail electrification on the Ryde-Shanklin line was ever considered.

Further details of the proposed electrification plans were revealed to the press in July 1966 and summed up briefly by *The Times*:

'The eight-and-a-half miles of railway between Ryde pierhead and Shanklin, Isle of Wight, is to be electrified at a cost of £500,000 by next Easter. London Underground trains, repainted blue, will be used on the line.'[41]

The *County Press* had rather more details. Work was soon to begin on the building of substations and installation of conductor rails and new fencing, and the line would be closed completely for approximately ten weeks in the New Year in order to allow for all works to be completed in time to launch the new electric service by Easter 1966. Work on the 'new' trains was already under way and the Minister of Transport had stated that it would be 'reasonable for British Rail to consider increasing fares … so as to reduce, if not to eliminate, the loss which is expected to be incurred on the new service.'[42]

The Standard Stock

The 'new' trains being prepared for the Isle of Wight were London Underground's so-called 'Standard Stock'. Having been built by several different manufacturers over a period of more than a decade from 1923 onwards, these trains presented a somewhat less than 'standard' appearance and by the mid-1960s were already around forty years old. Some were barely younger than some of the loco-hauled stock they would be replacing on the Island. Considered life-expired by London Transport, the trains were being withdrawn for scrap as new stock was introduced, so were readily available for sale to British Rail. Having first made enquiries as far back as 1961, BR initially acquired twelve Standard Stock cars during 1964; this would have been enough to operate the shuttle service from Ryde Pier Head to Ryde St John's if the rest of the network had closed as planned at the time. By January 1965, with the future of the Isle of Wight's remaining lines still undecided, London Transport was storing sixty-one withdrawn cars at Ruislip depot, at BR's expense, in addition to the twelve cars already held by BR and now stored at Micheldever. Collectively this would have been enough to operate the Ryde-Ventnor and Ryde-Cowes lines if the Minister of Transport decided to save the entire Isle of Wight network. With the Minister's announcement in July 1965 that only Ryde-Shanklin would be retained, it was determined that only forty-six cars would be required. When the cost of refurbishing the cars proved higher than expected, this figure was reduced to just forty-three cars; these would be marshalled into six four-car sets and six three-car sets, together with one spare Driving Motor Car (the original intention had been to have a spare four-car set). Since six seven-car sets would be required to provide the intended five-trains-per-hour peak summer Saturday service, this meant that forty-two cars out of forty-three would need to be in operation at once.

Numbering

The SR had a long tradition of using alpha-numeric codes to describe its electric multiple units (4-SUB = 4-car SUBurban unit, 5-BEL = 5-car Brighton BELle unit, etc),

and the new Isle of Wight sets were classified accordingly. The four-car sets (later to become Class 485) became 4-VEC while the three-car sets (later to be Class 486) were 3-TIS. Individually these abbreviations meant nothing, but coupled together to form a seven-car set for the peak summer service they became 'VECTIS' – the Roman name for the Isle of Wight. The VEC units were numbered in the sequence 041-046 and the TIS units 031-036. Initially it seems to have been the intention that seven-car trains would consist of numerically matched units (031+041, 032+042, etc) but in practice this quickly proved unrealistic and it appears likely it was abandoned after the first summer of electric operation.

Individual cars were numbered (with some gaps) as follows: Driving Motors (DMs) 1-25; Control Trailers (CTs) 26-36; Trailers 41-49 and 92-96. The break in the Trailer numbering is largely accounted for by the numbers 51-62 and 71-86 already being taken by Waterloo & City Line stock, while other gaps are only partly explained by the last-minute decision to reduce the planned fleet size from forty-six to forty-three cars. Each 3-TIS unit included a CT at the Ryde end and a DM at the Shanklin end, while the 4-VEC sets had DMs at both ends, meaning that a seven-car VEC-TIS formation would always include three DMs. The DMs chosen for the Isle of Wight dated from between 1927 and 1934, while the CTs were built in 1925 (save for one 1927 example) and the Trailers in 1923. Four of the CTs were to be used as Trailers only.[43]

Car numbers were originally applied in the format S11S; the 'S' prefix indicated a vehicle allocated to the Southern Region, while the 'S' suffix (later dropped) was that usually applied to pre-nationalisation vehicles inherited by BR from the Southern Railway in 1948. Obviously that was not technically the case on this occasion, but clearly BR had never previously needed to come up with a suffix to cover the circumstance of vehicles acquired from London Underground!

'A' ends and 'D' ends

Because of the non-reversible nature of the couplings in the Standard Stock, all driving vehicles were designated either 'A' ends or 'D' ends and could only be coupled together A+D, never A+A or D+D. This would prove no problem for the Isle of Wight, where there was no means of turning the cars anyway; all 'A' ends were marshalled to face towards Ryde and all 'D' ends towards Shanklin. Since the 4-VEC units were to have DMs at both ends and the 3-TIS units had DMs at the southern end only, this meant that just six (operational) Control Trailers were required – all of which were north-facing 'A' ends. Conversely there were to be nineteen DMs on the Island (including one spare), of which almost two-thirds were south-facing 'D' ends. The spare vehicle was DM No S10S, which was a north-facing 'A' end – meaning that there were no spare south-facing driving vehicles of any type.

In service the 4-VEC units were intended to operate alone during the winter months while the 3-TIS units were to be attached to the southern end to form a seven-car

VEC-TIS formation in the summer months. In practice this meant that a north-facing CT of a TIS unit was almost always coupled to the south-facing DM of a VEC unit and, until the late 1980s, were rarely seen at the front of a train – something that is clearly borne out by the photographic evidence. Cab fronts were usually lettered 'A' or 'D' – although clearly the distinction would have been obvious simply from the direction they were facing.

Livery

The 'blue' colour scheme referred to in the *Times* quote above was BR's new Corporate Rail Blue livery, launched in 1965. All of the Isle of Wight vehicles were repainted in this livery at Stewarts Lane Depot prior to their transfer to the Island, making them the first complete fleet of 'new' trains to be launched into service in this livery (probably not what the designers had in mind when they created BR's new 'modern' image!). As such the vehicles were in all-over blue with grey roofs, brown underframes and full yellow ends. On the DMs the yellow of the front ends extended around the side to include the cabside door – a rare early example of wrap-round yellow ends on BR rolling stock – while double-arrow logos were placed midway up the blue area of the cabside. As mentioned above, the Control Trailers at the Ryde end of the 3-TIS units were rarely used as driving vehicles; these received no double-arrows, and the yellow end was not wrapped round as far as the cab door. The CTs that were used as Trailer Cars received no yellow ends.

All cars were electrically overhauled, including conversion from fourth-rail to third-rail supply, at London Transport's Acton Works before being transferred to Stewarts Lane for cosmetic refurbishment. This included an internal as well as external repaint, although the LT seating moquette was originally retained in the majority

of vehicles. The *County Press* reported that 'British Rail have modified the Tube train carriages to allow more space for passengers'[44] although the reality was that a number of seats had been removed, three in the Driving Motors and six in the Trailers and Control Trailers, to provide room for luggage racks. Accommodation was 2nd Class only (1st Class having been abolished on the Island's railways in January 1966), and no provision was included for the carrying of mail, which in future was to be distributed throughout the Island by road.

Arrival on the Island

The first tube vehicle to arrive on the Isle of Wight was Control Trailer S38S (subsequently renumbered S26S), which was transported by a Pickfords lorry, via the Portsmouth-Fishbourne ferry, on 1 September 1966. On the same day it was offloaded onto Island rails for the first time via a ramp at Ryde St John's depot with the aid of Class 'O2' No W24 *Calbourne* and a match wagon converted from an ex-LBSCR van. Three days later the same formation worked to Shanklin and back as a clearance trial designed in part to test the difference in platform height between the stations and the new trains. The fact that air brakes had long been fitted as standard to Isle of Wight locomotives, unlike their vacuum-fitted counterparts on the mainland, meant that No W24 was able to supply air not only for the tube car's brakes but also for the operation of a set of doors. With hindsight it seems strangely appropriate that *Calbourne*, destined to become the flagship locomotive of the Isle of Wight Steam Railway, should have been chosen for such a historic run – possibly the only occasion on which a tube car was hauled by steam along the length of the line. At the time, however, no one could have predicted that this particular locomotive was destined to outlive its 'modern' replacement.

The first tube vehicle to arrive on the Isle of Wight was Control Trailer No S38S on 1 September 1966. Intended to form part of 3-TIS No 037, the subsequent decision to reduce the planned fleet size from forty-six to forty-three vehicles would see it quickly renumbered as car S26S of 3-TIS No 031. On 4 September the newly arrived vehicle is seen at Shanklin forming part of a gauging test train hauled by No W24 *Calbourne. J. Mackett, IWSR Archive*

As part of the gauging trails conducted on 4 September, the height difference between platform and tube car was measured, as shown here at Ryde St John's Road. Cost-cutting measures would eventually see a height difference of up to 9 inches deemed acceptable at all stations south of Ryde Esplanade. *IWSR Archive*

4-VEC unit No 043 passes through Clapham Junction on a test run in the autumn of 1966. The 1950s-built BR Standard Class 2 tank engine behind is considerably younger than the tube cars but, with the end of Southern Region steam less than a year away, is likely destined for scrap. Had things turned-out differently it might have been these locomotives, rather than tube trains, that made the journey across the Solent. *R. Mason, Colour-Rail.com*

Driving Motor No S22S of 4-VEC No 042 makes its arrival on the Isle of Wight as it disembarks at Fishbourne from the MV *Camber Queen* on 21 December 1966. The additional weight of the DMs meant that two Pickfords tractors had to be used to haul the low-loaders on and off the ferries. *BR(S) Official, IWSR Archive*

1 January 1967: the day after the end of steam. LBSCR Brake 3rd No S4168 faces up to one of its 'modern' replacements in the form of Standard Stock trailer No S46S. Only one year separates these vehicles in age, S46S dating from 1923 while S4168 was built in 1922, albeit on a pre-war underframe. Despite the painted slogans, this would not be 'The End' for No S4168, which survives today in regular service on the Isle of Wight Steam Railway. No S46S would not be so lucky, being cut up at Sandown in 1989. *A. Blackburn, IWSR Archive*

The end of steam

From this point on the end of steam came quickly. The end of the summer timetable on 17 September 1966 saw the last ever steam-hauled passenger train on Ryde Pier. From the next day onward the railway pier was closed for reconstruction work, as it had been for most winters since 1963; this time it would not see passengers again until the electric service was inaugurated in the spring of 1967. The closure of the pier coincided with the temporary closure of the down line through Ryde Tunnel, meaning that all services north of Ryde St John's now had to be top-and-tailed to Ryde Esplanade. This in turn allowed work to begin on lifting the trackbed and raising the tunnel floor; this was an anti-flooding measure intended to take advantage of the fact that the tube trains would require less clearance than their predecessors. Crucially this reduced the already limited loading gauge in the tunnel from 13ft 6in to 12ft 3½in, seemingly guaranteeing that the Ryde-Shanklin line would be restricted to tube trains for the foreseeable future. The tunnel floor under the up line would be raised accordingly in the New Year after steam services had ceased.

After 102 years the final steam-hauled passenger service on the Ryde-Shanklin line departed from Shanklin for Ryde St John's Road in the cold evening gloom of 31 December 1966. This would be the last passenger train on the Isle of Wight for almost three months. Only two steam locomotives officially remained in service beyond that date, Nos W24 *Calbourne* and W31 *Chale* being retained until March to

assist with electrification works alongside newly arrived Hunslet diesel shunter No D2554. Two other serviceable locomotives are noted to have been steamed in early 1967, with No W27 *Merstone* recorded as being the very last Island loco steamed by BR, shunting eight of its condemned sisters into the Freshwater yard at Newport on 18 April, just days before its own scrapping. In May 1967 the sale of No W24 to the Wight Locomotive Society would mark the start of another chapter in the history of the Island's railways, albeit outside the scope of this book.

Electrification works

For the hundreds of enthusiasts who flocked to the Island to witness steam's last rites on New Year's Eve 1966, much evidence of electrification was already on show, with conductor rails in place at the southern end of the line and newly arrived tube trains already stored on the down line between Ryde St John's Road and Smallbrook Junction. Much more work would follow over the next three months.

Three substations would be required to serve the electric railway, with the *County Press* reporting on 10 December that one had already been completed at Ryde St John's. Two more were to be built at Rowborough and Sandown. The same article also noted that wholesale delivery of tube cars was now under way, using a 'special bridging device' to transfer the vehicles on and off the Portsmouth to Fishbourne ferry 'almost every day between now and Christmas.'[45]

An unidentified tube car makes its way carefully along Argyle Street, Ryde, on the back of a low-loader en route from the ferry terminal at Fishbourne to the depot at Ryde St John's Road. With forty-three tube vehicles arriving on the Island during the winter of 1966/67, this must have become a familiar sight to local residents.
F. E. J. Ward, Derek Gawn collection

One day after its arrival at Fishbourne, car No S22S is carefully manoeuvred into the yard at Ryde St John's Road on 22 December 1966. *J. Mackett, IWSR Archive*

In December 1966, with the end of steam rapidly approaching, 'O2' Class tank engine No W16 *Ventnor* stands in the loco shed at Ryde. Two further 'O2s' can be seen at the back of the shed, but beside No W16 sits an imposter in the shape of a newly arrived tube carriage in BR blue livery. *A. Gray, Colour-Rail.com*

Infrastructure changes to accommodate the new trains were kept to a minimum. Ideally platform heights needed to be adjusted to allow for the lower floors of the tube trains; this was achieved at Ryde Pier Head by raising the track level and at Ryde Esplanade, where the platforms extend partly over land and partly over sea, by lowering the platforms. Further down the line savings were made by not carrying out this work, leaving instead a 9-inch step down from platform to train floor.

At Ryde Pier Head the station was remodelled from its 1930s four-platform layout to just two tracks and three platform faces. The former Platform 1, on the easternmost side of the station, was taken out of use in early 1966 and for the start of services in 1967 the remaining Platforms 2, 3 and 4 were renumbered 1, 2 and 3 (so that the former Platform 2 became the new Platform 1, etc). The new Platform 2 was widened so that Platforms 1 and 2 now faced on to either side of the same track, allowing passengers to join trains from one side and alight from the other in order to speed up loading. Unfortunately the canopy over Platform 2 was not widened, meaning that passengers were now exposed to the elements when boarding the train. The new Platform 3 was intended to mainly see

This early view of the new Platform 2 at Ryde Pier Head is undated, but note that the two staff members are still wearing the uniforms of the steam era. The driver on the right is Ken West, a former steam driver who drove the first revenue-earning Isle of Wight tube train on 20 March 1967. On retirement from BR in 1994 Mr West would return to steam once more, regularly driving his former loco No W24 *Calbourne* on the Isle of Wight Steam Railway. *Kevin Robertson, Crécy Transport Archive*

use at peak times when two trains were in the station. (Just to confuse matters, 20 years later the platforms would be renumbered in the opposite direction so that Platforms 3 and 1 swapped identities.)

Elsewhere the stations, track layouts and signalling were to remain almost entirely unchanged from steam days. All stations retained two operational platform faces. Five signal boxes, at Ryde Pier Head, Ryde St John's Road, Brading, Sandown and Shanklin, remained in situ and in use, together with a 1966-built ground frame box at Ryde Esplanade. The former box at Smallbrook was replaced by a panel in Ryde St John's box. Signals remained largely semaphore although a special version of tokenless block signalling was developed to replace the former single-line tokens. The line remained fully double-tracked between Ryde Pier Head and Smallbrook Junction – unlike in steam days the Ryde St John's to Smallbrook section would now be worked as a fully double-tracked section all year round instead of just for the summer months – and also between Brading and Sandown. This latter section had been doubled by the Southern Railway in the 1920s.

Cosmetically, 'modernisation' was largely limited to the installation of new signage in BR's new black-on-white corporate style at Ryde Pier Head; further down the line the pre-nationalisation 'target' signboards of the Southern Railway reigned supreme. All stations retained the old green-and-cream colour scheme. This was not, to use a modern phrase, total route modernisation.

A view of Shanklin during the first summer of electric services reveals how little had changed since the steam era, despite the cessation of services to Ventnor. Both tracks are electrified and Platform 2 remains in use complete with waiting shelter and signal box – the roof of the latter is just visible over the canopy. The 'D'-end car of 4-VEC No 042 seen here is the original No S15S, which would be withdrawn following accident damage in October 1967 and replaced with another car of the same number in 1971. *Nick Doolan collection*

In another view of Shanklin, this time taken from Platform 2 on 18 August 1968, 4-VEC unit No 045 is seen at the rear of a seven-car formation shunting forward across Landguard Road Bridge. From the headshunt it will access Platform 2 in order to form the next northbound service to Ryde. This manoeuvre was only necessary during the peak summer season when a 12-minute-interval service was in operation. *Nick Doolan collection*

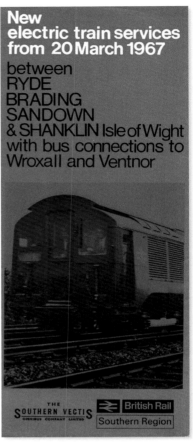

New electric train services from 20 March 1967

between
RYDE
BRADING
SANDOWN
& SHANKLIN Isle of Wight
with bus connections to
Wroxall and Ventnor

THE SOUTHERN VECTIS OMNIBUS COMPANY LIMITED | British Rail Southern Region

Above: 4-VEC No 045 waits at Ryde St John's Road forming a northbound service in the 1960s. The steam locomotive shed, demolished in late 1969, is still present on the left, and a Southern Railway 'target' sign (carrying the shortened name 'Ryde St. Johns') can be seen on the lamp post. Note the red disc on the rear of the train; these repainted steam-era headcode discs were carried on the rear of the Island's Standard Stock in lieu of a red marker light. *Nick Doolan collection*

Right: A British Rail timetable leaflet publicising the new electrified services, which were to begin on 20 March 1967. *Author's collection*

Entry into service

On Saturday 4 March 1967 the *County Press* reported:

> 'Proving trials of electric trains on the Island began on Wednesday over all but about a mile of the eight-and-a-half miles of the new electrified railway between Ryde pier head and Shanklin.'[46]

The article went on to detail how reporters and officials had witnessed the official 'switch-on' at 1.20pm, having waited since 11.00am, and that 10 minutes later a four-car train had made the first of several short runs towards the Esplanade (presumably not getting very far as the tunnel under Ryde was still closed for maintenance). Subsequently the unit travelled south to Shanklin and back – demonstrating 'the rapid acceleration familiar to all who have travelled on the London Underground system' and attracting 'considerable interest among occupiers of lineside houses.' If this was a publicity exercise it appears to have been successful.

One regular observer of the Island's railway scene at this time was Derek Gawn, who noted further testing under way on 8 March 1967 and records that test runs appear to have become an almost daily event from then until the official launch into service. Increasingly these test trains became unofficially open to the public; Derek himself travelled on many of them – recording a speed of 53mph at Morton Common on 11 March – and recalls that 'towards the end test runs were often carrying 20 or 30 interested spectators'. On 10 March diesel shunter No D2554 travelled to the Pier Head with six bolster wagons, a match truck and an unidentified tube car – making possibly the first recorded appearance of a tube vehicle on Ryde Pier. Within the next five days the third-rail up the pier was switched on; 4-VEC No 041 was recorded travelling from Ryde St John's Road to the Pier Head at 16.45 on 15 March.

After eleven weeks with no service, passenger trains finally returned to the Ryde-Shanklin line with the 07.18 departure from Ryde Pier Head on Monday 20 March 1967. The initial service saw just one train an hour until 20 May, when the full summer timetable of three departures per hour on weekdays (two for Shanklin and one terminating at Sandown) and the maximum five trains an hour Saturday service from Ryde to Shanklin began. The first day of service also saw a special inaugural run carrying invited guests depart from the Pier Head at 12.18.

All public trains on the first day were operated by either 4-VEC No 041 or 3-TIS No 031, the latter operating in a four-car formation with the addition of spare DM No S10S, while the then regular Sandown Grammar School train was a seven-car VEC-TIS formation consisting of units Nos 032 and 044. The formation of the 'inaugural' special is unrecorded, but was most likely also formed of Nos 032 and 044. For the remainder of the month it appears that all services were operated by a combination of just five units, Nos 031 (operating as a four-car set), 032, 041, 042 and 044.

20 March 1967: the first day of passenger services on the newly electrified Ryde-Shanklin line. 4-VEC unit No 041 arrives at Ryde St John's Road station forming the 11.59 Shanklin-Ryde Pier Head service, while 3-TIS No 031, which operated that day as a four-car unit with the addition of DM No S10S, occupies the siding in the former Platform 3. 4-VEC No 042 stands outside the depot. Note that the down platform still retained a full-length canopy in 1967, although this would not last much longer. *Alastair McIntyre, IWSR Archive*

4-VEC unit No 045 is seen here on test at Weybridge on the mainland on 28 March 1967 – more than a week after electric services had launched on the Isle of Wight. A full complement of vehicles was not required at Ryde until the peak summer service launched on 20 May that year. *Colour-Rail.com*

Inaugural lunch

On arrival at Shanklin the guests from the 'inaugural' train enjoyed lunch at a Shanklin hotel where they were addressed by Southern Region General Manager David McKenna. As reported in the *County Press*, Mr McKenna's speech was a robust defence of British Rail's policy towards the Island. The Island's railways had 'certain peculiarities' that had made it 'physically impossible to continue with the system as they knew it'. The old rolling stock had needed replacing and the 'structure gauge' was 'rather smaller than that on any other part of British Rail'. Electrifying the line was 'the most economical and attractive way of continuing the railway' and any talk of the new trains being 'scrap stock' was dismissed as merely referring to the price BR had paid: 'I can assure you that it has had a complete and thorough rebuild and that there is a lot of life in that stock.' As it turned out the new trains would need to have rather more life in them than Mr McKenna probably anticipated at the time.

Mr McKenna defended fare increases and noted that the 'fundamental economic problem' presented by the Island's railways was the fault of the 'very high peak in summer' (i.e. the tourist trade) and not Islanders themselves. Skirting around the fact that BR had only recently been fighting to close the line, he concluded:

> 'If this new renaissant railway may seem a little unconventional and may have emerged in rather an unexpected form … behind it is a great will on the part of the Southern to do a good job for the Island, and at the same time fulfil our obligations to the taxman.'[47]

Reaction

So, was the new service a success? Many Islanders had been demanding modernisation for several years – how did they react when 'modernisation' turned out to mean 40-year-old tube trains?

As far back as 1964, when news first broke that BR was considering old tube trains for possible use on Ryde Pier, one *County Press* reader had drawn an unfavourable comparison with the 'fast, comfortable, silver streamlined electric trains' on Southend Pier, saying, 'So this is what they think of us! The worst is good enough for the Isle of Wight.'[48] The 1966 revelation that the tube trains were to be operated over the whole of the Ryde-Shanklin line brought forward further readers' complaints about the 'out-worn, unsaleable and unsuitable Underground rolling stock off the junk heap.'[49] The MP was similarly unimpressed: 'If that was the Government's idea of modernisation, it was small wonder that production in this country was stagnant.'[50]

Despite the initial reaction, the actual entry into service of the 'new' trains seems to have been largely successful. One *County Press* reader who travelled on the first day wrote to commend 'improved timing (20 minutes against 27); space comfort, cleanliness, cheaper (return) … these new trains give a much quicker journey.'[51] Four months later, with the peak summer service in operation, BR's Island rail manager Reginald Streeter was confident enough to predict that the new service would make more money than the old steam trains. Speaking to the *County Press*, he stated that on the first Saturday of the summer peak 124 trains had operated between Ryde and Shanklin with only a 5-minute delay caused by a temporary signal failure reducing efficiency to 93%. ('Normally Island trains run 100 per cent on time'!)[52]

'Sticking doors'

While expressing his satisfaction with the first four months of operation, Mr Streeter did admit to 'minor annoyances such as sticking doors'. (This would not have come as a surprise to Londoners, for whom sticking doors on tube trains have always been an issue.) Despite this issue the use of air-operated sliding doors was one area in which the elderly Standard Stock (the first tube cars to feature automatic doors) might genuinely be said to have been 'modern' at a time when such an innovation was largely unheard of on the BR network, save for a few pockets of electrified suburban networks. On the mainland the Southern Region would continue to build slam-door stock based on the 1950s Mark 1 coach design until the early 1970s. On the Island the combination of open saloons and automatic doors made the new trains a radical step-change from the compartment stock they replaced. Passengers travelling on the ferry from Ryde would not see any trains with automatic doors in regular passenger service at Portsmouth Harbour until 1988 – and then only on trains to Cardiff – more than two decades after the introduction of the Standard Stock on the Isle of Wight.

Overall the new electric service was a success. The seven-car trains provided in the summer were longer, by one coach, than their steam predecessors. The 'new' trains were also faster, cleaner and generally more reliable. The five-trains-an-hour service on summer Saturdays was probably the most frequent that the Ryde-Shanklin line had ever seen; certainly it has never been bettered since. In 1970 the Island's MP conceded that the new trains 'did provide a good, regular service more economically than steam trains.'[53]

Ventnor

Undoubtedly the most keenly felt of the 1966 Beeching closures was the loss of the railway from Shanklin to Ventnor. From the outset it was the Ryde-Ventnor line that the County Council and MP had fought hard to save; any defence of the Cowes line by the Island authorities had been lukewarm by comparison. In 1963 Alderman Woodnutt MP stated that closure of the line to Sandown, Shanklin *and Ventnor* would take place 'over my dead body'[54]. When it was announced in 1965 that the line would be reprieved only as far Shanklin he celebrated that the 'main objective' had been achieved, but added that 'it is quite clear from the studies we have made that a modernised line could not be economically viable, unless it runs all the way to Ventnor.'[55] BR thought otherwise and, despite Alderman Woodnutt's personal appeal in

A rare instance of the Isle of Wight living up to its name! Control Trailer No S26S, the 'A' end of 3-VEC No 031, stands in the snowy wastes of the Up Yard at Ryde St John's Road on 10 December 1967. Wintry weather remains a hazard for the Ryde-Shanklin line, owing to the absence of either snowploughs or point heaters. *J. Mackett, IWSR Archive*

February 1966 to Barbara Castle, the new Minister of Transport, closure of the Shanklin-Ventnor section went ahead as planned in April. By December the Ventnor Hotels Association was reporting an estimated 25% drop in trade against previous years (mainly due to a drop in casual trade as most visitors were apparently unaware the railway south of Shanklin had closed until they actually arrived on the Island).[56]

During 1966 a campaign to retain and electrify the railway, but only as far as Wroxall, received a small amount of coverage in the *County Press* ('It is felt in the town that the station could be renamed Ventnor and this would dispense with the cost of maintaining the tunnel which ran into the old Ventnor Town station'[57]), but came to nothing. In January 1967 the County Council announced that it was making formal approaches to both BR and the Ministry of Transport regarding electrification of the line throughout to Ventnor 'in the light of fresh circumstances since the original closure was announced.'[58] At the celebratory lunch held to launch the new service in March 1967, these approaches were addressed by the Southern Region's General Manager, who stated that it was a matter for the Minister but in his opinion would cost around £100,000: 'This would not be just a marginal extension; it would require

the building of a new substation and the provision of at least one more full seven-coach train.'[59]

As late as the autumn of 1968 *Wight Report*, the newsletter of the Wight Locomotive Society (WLS), announced that 'The battle for the Ventnor line is still not over!' as the Parliamentary Secretary for the Minister of Transport had agreed with the County Council to review the situation again. However, by now it was becoming clear that, if Islanders wanted the line reopened, they would likely have to pay for it themselves: 'If Ventnor fights hard enough to impress the Ministry, and is prepared to subsidise the project...'[60]

In the end it was both the cost and a lack of suitable extra rolling stock that probably scuppered all hopes of reopening to Ventnor. The only withdrawn Standard Stock cars that London Underground had available were those that BR had rejected first time around, and in the meantime their condition had deteriorated further. Track-lifting between Shanklin and Ventnor took place in 1970 (some of the trackwork at Wroxall had been reportedly lifted as far back as September 1966[61]), with ownership of the trackbed transferred to the County Council shortly afterwards. Wroxall station was demolished in July 1971 and demolition of Ventnor began on 16 January 1972, the latter work being undertaken by a member of the WLS.[62]

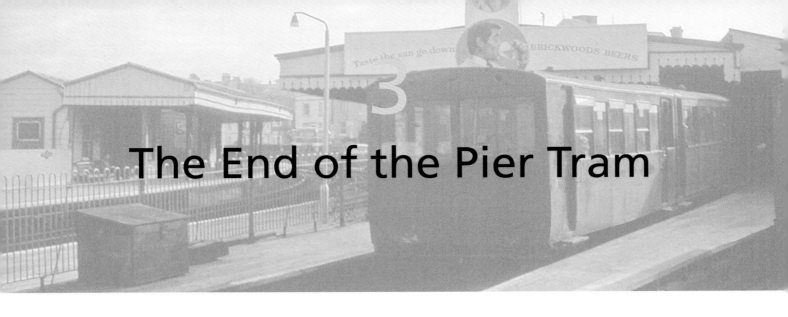

The End of the Pier Tram

Surprisingly perhaps, when electric services started running in 1967, the Ryde to Shanklin line wasn't the only double-tracked standard-gauge British Rail service operating along the length of Ryde Pier. It wasn't even the oldest railway service on the pier; that title belonged to the Ryde Pier Tramway, which by that time had been in operation for more than a century.

History and operation

Opened in 1864, and taken into railway ownership by the Southern Railway in 1924, the Ryde Pier Tramway had at various times been operated by steam, horse, electric, diesel and petrol-driven motive power. At one time, before the mainland railway companies had funded the extension of the Shanklin line northward from Ryde

St John's Road to the Pier Head, the Pier Tram had even snaked as far south as St John's Road station to form an end-on connection with the Island's railways. By the time the tube trains arrived in 1967 the tramway was being operated by Motor Cars Nos 1 and 2, built for petrol operation in 1927 and converted to diesel power in 1959/60, working with Trailer Cars Nos 7 and 8, constructed in the late 1930s. The connecting pointwork between the two tracks of the tramway had been removed in Southern Railway days, meaning that the two tramlines were entirely separate from each other, as well as from the adjacent railway tracks. Motor Car No 1 operated with Trailer No 8 on the eastern track, while Motor Car No 2 and Trailer No 7 served the western track.

Motor Car No 1 leads Trailer No 8 down the pier on 30 December 1966. Alongside it reconstruction of Ryde Pier Head railway station for the new electric services due to begin in March 1967 is already well under way. *G. S. Cocks, Colour-Rail.com*

In this 1960s view of the interior of the Pier Head tramway station, the signal box on the railway pier, demolished in the 1970s, can be seen in the centre, while on the left of it a steam crane appears to be in operation, suggesting that reconstruction of the railway is in progress. *IWSR Archive*

Motor Car No 2 propels luggage truck No 9 along the pier on 13 June 1964. No 9, seen here carrying a pram and a number of suitcases, was the only luggage trolley and was usually confined to the western track. *A. Blackburn, IWSR Archive*

The interior of Ryde Esplanade tramway station was photographed just days before closure in January 1969. Motor Car No 1 can be seen with Trailer No 8 in the eastern platform awaiting the next call of duty. *David A. Lawrence, Colour-Rail.com*

The final years

It might surprise some readers to learn that the trams, a prominent feature of Ryde Pier throughout the steam age, actually survived the end of steam at all. Given that it was probably only the sheer volume of foot passengers arriving and departing on the ferries on summer Saturdays that forced British Rail to retain the Ryde-Shanklin line, it is interesting to note that in 1967 it was apparently felt that the newly modernised railway might still not have the capacity to handle the traffic on Ryde Pier on its own. Nonetheless, unlike the railway, for the pier tramway there was to be no new investment.

Despite the fact that the tramcars were in some cases younger than the 'new' electric trains operating on the neighbouring tracks, the ageing vehicles, which remained in Southern Region green without a hint of a double-arrow logo to be seen, must have seemed like a survivor from another age. In July 1967, in an otherwise glowing review of the new electric train services, British Rail's Isle of Wight Manager would admit to only one complaint from passengers: 'Mr Streeter said one sore point for many people was that there were apparently no plans for the replacement of the old pier trams at Ryde.'[63] Clearly time was running out for the Ryde Pier Tramway.

In July 1968 *Wight Report*, the newsletter of the Wight Locomotive Society, reported to its readers that 'It is likely that the 1968 Summer Season will be the last for the Drewry trams which operate on Ryde Pier.'[64] This was despite the fact that a recent repaint of Ryde Pier Head station into the latest British Rail colours had included a full repaint for the adjacent tramway station! Finally in December 1968 BR announced that the tram would be closed from 27 January 1969, with the last services to run on Sunday 26th.

In the end the fate of the pier tram had been sealed by a combination of a factors that had led passengers to defect from the tram to the railway. Surprising though it may seem to modern readers, the replacement of steam traction with second-hand tube trains had made the railway a more attractive option to many travellers at a time when an obvious lack of investment was making the tram cars ('visibly in poor condition'[65]) seem like a definite second choice. Moreover, the coming of the electric trains in 1967 had seen a new fare structure for Ryde Pier under which, in order to bring tram fares in line with train fares, the cost of a single tram ticket had been increased by 200% from 2d to 6d. (In 1969 *Wight Report* noted, apparently without irony, 'The revised fare structure … has failed to save the tramway in the present economic climate.'[66])

The exterior of Ryde Pier Head tramway station is seen on 9 April 1964. A sign to the left of the entrance announces that the tram fare is 2d. In 1967 fares were raised by 200% to 6d in order to bring them in line with those on the newly electrified railway. *A. Blackburn, IWSR Archive*

Trailer No 8 stands with Motor Car No 1 behind it in the eastern tram station platform at Ryde Esplanade in January 1969. Trailer No 7 in the western platform is just visible on the right of the photo while on the left can be seen the railway station, still in green and cream colours. A Southern Railway 'target' can be glimpsed on the down platform. *David A. Lawrence, Colour-Rail.com*

January 1969 again, and the end is nigh. Photographed at Ryde Esplanade, the BR notice in the foreground reads 'From Monday 27 January 1969 the Ryde Pier Tramway service will be replaced by a shuttle electric train service between the Pier Head and Esplanade stations.' *David A. Lawrence, Colour-Rail.com*

Shuttle service

In order to facilitate the closure of the tramway a 'shuttle' train service was announced to be introduced on the pier consisting of one unit that would simply shuttle between the Pier Head and Esplanade stations. Intended to replace the service provided by the tramway, this would increase the frequency of trains on the pier but at the expense of services further down the line. Rolling stock was at a premium and the use of an extra train formation for the pier shuttle meant that the frequency of trains to Shanklin on a summer Saturday would in future be reduced from five an hour to just four, the first of many service reductions that would follow over the ensuing decades. In fact, the lack of a crossover at Ryde Esplanade meant that the shuttle trains, which would only serve the Pier Head and Esplanade, would for the time being be forced to continue empty to Ryde St John's Road and back on each run – causing one pair of contemporary commentators to note:

'It hardly seems logical to run the train empty to and from St John's Road when extra revenue could be collected from passengers who live near there or who want to make use of the car park there!'[67]

As we shall see in the next chapter, infrastructure rationalisation in the 1970s would soon allow the pier shuttle service to be further streamlined and remove the need to run empty trains to St John's.

Despite the announcement of the shuttle service, the imminent closure of the tramway did not go unopposed on the Island, with a number of local authorities protesting the decision. For example, on 11 January 1969 the *County Press* reported:

'Sandown-Shanklin Council on Tuesday voted un-animously in favour of a resolution proposed by Mr D. H. Price protesting at the decision of British Rail to discontinue the motor tram service on Ryde Pier... "We should be very concerned at the closure of this service which will cause great inconvenience to the people travelling to Sandown and Shanklin," said Mr Price... Referring to recent rough weather he pointed out that the electric trains had stopped running and to reach the boats passengers had had to use the trams. If the service was taken off what would have happened? He supposed they would have had to walk.'[68]

The fear that rough weather would prevent the trains from running was no idle scaremongering. The combination of high tides and high winds could cause waves to splash over the rails on the pier. This had presented no problems for the former steam trains, and nor did it present an issue for the diesel-driven trams, but for the newly electrified railway it was a different matter; the current along the pier had to be switched off and the trains cancelled. This remains a problem even today, and at the time of Mr Price's protest had occurred as recently as December 1968, leaving the trams, on two separate occasions, as the only means of accessing the boats just weeks before their abolition.[69]

The last day

Despite the protests from several local authorities, British Rail remained unwavering in its decision and the last day duly arrived, as advertised, on Sunday 26 January 1969. In fact, Motor Car No 1 had failed on the Saturday, leaving just Motor Car No 2 and Trailer No 7 on the western track to enact the final rites alone. Throughout the day a normal service operated with passenger numbers swollen by enthusiasts with cameras and recording equipment. Both vehicles acquired 'last day' embellishments as the day wore on; Derek Gawn records that Car No 2 was adorned with a laurel wreath at about 11.30am and bunting added at 9.00pm, while Trailer No 7 was decorated with the addition of a BR double-arrow flag across its front from lunchtime onwards. At 11.15pm 105 years of history were brought to a close when the last ever Ryde Pier tram departed from the Pier Head on its final journey back to the Esplanade station.

The *Isle of Wight County Press* chose to record the tramway's passing with a somewhat melodramatic piece, part obituary, part history, written as if in the words of the tram itself:

'Old horses never die … But old trams die. They die a horrible death in the breakers yard. Their bodies are torn apart timber by timber with hammer and axe, smashed into a million splinters in the jaws of a giant steel crusher…

Now those electric trains are going to step into our shoes because nobody wants a 42-year-old tram. If those trains fail to run when the weather gets bad do not shout for us. We might not be there.'[70]

With the *County Press* choosing to play on the emotional angle, it fell instead to *Wight Report* to take a more pragmatic, and surprisingly unsentimental, approach:

'As much as the closure is regretted, if this latest economy measure helps to retain the Shanklin line, is it not worthwhile?'[71]

Protest and acceptance

Needless to say, the ending of the pier tram service was not accepted without protest, and various local authorities and organisations continued to register complaints over

An early incarnation of the Ryde Pier shuttle, introduced following the closure of the pier tramway in 1969, is seen at Ryde Esplanade in the summer of 1972. At this stage the shuttle was still a timetabled service from Ryde Pier Head, and continued empty from Esplanade to St John's Road, via the down line, before regaining the up line and returning to the pier. Note the 'Ryde Only' headboard – actually a recycled steam headcode disc. *Nick Doolan collection*

the coming months and beyond. Within a few days of the closure, a report of a meeting of the Shanklin Hotel & Guest House Association noted:

'Mr A. Whitehead asked that a complaint be made as to the cessation of the Ryde Pier tram service and said that on the first night of the new service people wanting to get to Ryde Esplanade from the boat that arrived at 9.10pm had to wait 20 minutes for a train.'[72]

In April 1969 councillors at a meeting of the Isle of Wight Executive Council expressed concern that trains from the Esplanade were allegedly being held back to catch last-minute travellers, as the trams had once done. This, they feared, meant that the elderly and infirm were now being caught up in a dangerous scramble for the boat at the Pier Head.[73] That same month Sadler-Vectrail Ltd (of which more in the next chapter) made a perhaps somewhat opportunistic offer to operate one of their own vehicles up the tramway in lieu of the old trams.[74]

As late as November 1970 the Isle of Wight Federation of Ratepayers' & Residents' Associations was proposing to send a letter of 'strong protest' to BR at the closure of the tramway[75], but by this time the tramcars had been removed from the pier and the situation seems to have been largely accepted by Islanders. In January 1970, one year after closure, the Island's MP, Alderman Mark Woodnutt, had accepted the status quo:

'The member agreed he objected to the closure of the Ryde Pier tram service in the beginning but the public was for ever telling British Rail to put its house in order. There were two services up the pier, train and tram, and British Rail considered they could carry everyone on the train. He queried this but they had proved their point, even in the middle of the holiday season, and he had to withdraw his objection.'[76]

What happened next: the tram

When the final tram departed from Ryde Pier Head on 26 January 1969 it was proudly emblazoned with the letters 'IVTG' above the driver's windows. These were the initials of the Island Vintage Transport Group, whose members had been collecting funds on the tram throughout the day. Formed in January 1969 by a group of Wight Locomotive Society (WLS) members, it was the intention of the IVTG to save one of the tramcars for posterity, since it was beyond the means of the WLS itself to do so.

This aim seemed to have been achieved when, less than two months later, the County Press announced that Car No 2 had been purchased by the IVTG for the princely sum of £30 with the intention of moving it to Newport station, then occupied by the WLS, where 'It could then be used by the Vectrail Society … or placed in a museum which the Wight Locomotive Society intended to form'.[77] However, there was a catch. BR had apparently given the group an arbitrary eight-week timeslot, from 24 February, to remove the tramcar from the pier. Since this could only

be undertaken by crane, the group estimated that it would need to raise a further £100-150. Alarmingly the County Press noted:

'If this money could not be raised the only other way to move the tram would be by slicing it in half as the entrance to the pier was too small to allow it through in one piece. This would involve cutting the main beams and would detract from the appearance of the tram.'

Thankfully BR relented and Car No 2 remained on the tracks of the disused tramway for more than a year after closure. By this time, reported the County Press, the WLS had 'assumed control of the erstwhile Vintage Transport Group'[78]. Response to the IVTG's appeal had been 'very satisfactory', but the problems of removing the tramcar from the pier remained and in the end, while the vehicle was not sliced in half, it was a partially dismantled tram that was rescued from the pier on 21 February 1970, its bodywork removed for possible reassembly 'at a later date'. Car No 1 and the two trailers were still on the tram tracks at this stage and remained so for a further two months before being broken up for scrap.

Two years after its final trip down the pier, the County Press announced that the surviving tramcar had been restored to working order again at the WLS's Newport base 'and has been proved capable of moving carriages which are being restored for use at the society's projected Havenstreet steam railway centre.'[79] In reality, however, its bodywork still in storage, the 'tram' by this time was little more than a motorised chassis. The WLS's predicted move to Havenstreet finally took place at short notice on 24 January 1971, when all of its rolling stock travelled by rail to the new location over the course of six trips in the space of a single day. While four of those journeys were made by the society's then only locomotive, No W24 Calbourne, the other two trips – the first and the last on the day – were undertaken by the motorised remains of Car No 2. Thus it was that while Calbourne, rightly, carried the 'Last Train from Newport' headboard, it was actually a Ryde Pier tram, departing at around 8.50pm, that was the very last rail-borne vehicle to leave Newport station under its own power.

Initially the tramcar continued in operational use at Havenstreet, both for shunting moves and for the occasional passenger service. A few months after the move from Newport the County Press reported on the new Steam Railway's open days held over Whitsun 1971. In addition to steam haulage behind Calbourne, passengers had also been able to travel the Havenstreet-Wootton route on board the former pier tram 'especially equipped with temporary sides and seats … many took advantage of this novel means of seeing the line.'[80] Sadly the tram car's usefulness would soon be at an end. A few days after Whitsun a second steam locomotive arrived at Havenstreet, while just 12 months later the arrival of Spitfire, a Ruston & Hornsby diesel shunter, meant that the tram was no longer required for maintenance works. Noted the County Press:

The chassis of Ryde Pier Tramway Motor Car No 2, complete with the 'temporary sides and seats' described in the *County Press*, is seen carrying passengers at Wootton on the Isle of Wight Steam Railway in 1971. *Derek Gawn*

'The former Ryde Pier tram will now be retired from permanent way duties and will be stored until such time as it can be rebuilt to its former state in passenger use.'[81]

This temporary retirement of the tram would prove to be much longer than anyone could have imagined.

What happened next: the tramway
The structure known as Ryde Pier actually consists of three separate piers joined only at the Esplanade and Pier Head, and the position of the tramway pier, sandwiched between the promenade/vehicle pier and the railway pier, has ensured its continued survival long after the tracks it was built to carry. The former tramway station at the Pier Head was demolished in late 1970 to be replaced by a Trinity House Pilot Station, which sat upon the remains of the former platforms. A somewhat temporary-looking structure, this survived until the mid-1990s before being removed together with the foundations on which it once stood. Removal of the tramway tracks began in August 1971, with *Wight Report* noting that 'By early September, approximately half of the distance (both lines) had been removed.'[82] (The parallel steel girders, which can to this day be seen stretching along the

full length of the old tramway pier, are the structure on which the tracks once stood, not the tracks themselves.)

The existence of a disused route up the middle of Ryde Pier has proved itself useful as a diversionary route for the promenade pier on more than one occasion. In 1973 the pier experienced one of the most dramatic incidents in its history when the British Rail ferry MV *Shanklin* misjudged its approach in thick fog in the early hours of 9 March and succeeded in completely severing the promenade pier. Mr R. C. Streeter, BR's Island Manager, advised the *County Press*:

'The *Shanklin* struck the western side of the pier, about 150 yards from the pierhead, ploughing through the promenade part into the old tram track which stood up to the shock and left the electric railway undamaged.'

Miraculously no one was hurt in the collision. Many ferry passengers thought it was all 'a bit of a giggle'[83] although this was probably not an opinion shared by the occupants of a taxi, who had to swim for safety after plunging through the unexpected gap and into the sea. The possible consequences if the errant ferry had succeeded in severing the railway pier in the path of an oncoming train do not bear thinking about.

The damage caused to Ryde Pier by the stern of the MV *Shanklin* in the early hours of Friday 9 March 1973 can be clearly seen in this view taken on what is believed to be Saturday the 10th. The photographer is facing north up the promenade pier, which has been completely severed, while the workmen on the right are on the disused tramway pier, which withstood the collision. The proximity of the signal box on the railway pier can be clearly seen. *Derek Gawn*

The severing of the promenade pier left thirty-six cars marooned at the Pier Head. Taken on the same day as the previous image, this view shows one of these cars being carefully craned onto the deck of the MV *Fishbourne*, to be returned to dry land at the car ferry terminal of the same name. *Derek Gawn*

Taken on 5 July 2015 from an almost identical angle to the picture on page 33, this view shows what little remains of the Esplanade tramway station today. To the left Island Line unit No 006 departs from the Esplanade as the 16.07 service from Ryde Pier Head to Shanklin. *Martyn Hilbert*

With the promenade pier closed to traffic (thirty-six cars left stranded at the pier head were craned onto a car ferry the following day) the race was on to reopen in time for the Easter rush. For the first time the redundant tramway pier proved its worth as an alternative route, with *Wight Report* noting 'a short length of new decking for motor vehicles has been constructed over the former Tramway Pier immediately adjacent to the Signal Box.'[84]

Almost three decades later the tramway pier would become useful again when the promenade pier was once more closed to vehicular traffic after a routine inspection revealed extensive corrosion in August 2010. On this occasion the promenade pier would remain closed to all vehicles for eight months, but the need to carry out repairs would see pedestrians diverted onto a temporary walkway laid along the entire length of the old pier tramway from October 2010 until April 2011. Perhaps surprisingly, this potentially useful alternative route was closed and the decking removed once the promenade pier reopened.

One more permanent use for the former pier tramway was considered in July 2003 when the Wightlink company (inheritors of the former railway-owned ferry routes to the Island) applied for permission to lay a vehicle deck along the old tramway with a view to adapting the pier head for car ferries.[85] In the event nothing was to come of this proposal and, with the ferry terminal at Fishbourne since

In 2014 the Isle of Wight Steam Railway unveiled a blue plaque at the site of the Esplanade tram station to commemorate 150 years since the opening of the Ryde Pier Tramway. Facing onto the vehicle pier, the plaque can be viewed by pedestrians as they walk down the pier. *Author*

enlarged, it seems that the old tramway pier is likely to remain in its current rusting and unwanted state for the foreseeable future.

The tramcar recreation project

When tramcar No 2 (or at least what was left of it) was retired from operational use at Havenstreet in 1972, it was hoped that this would only be a temporary period of storage until such time as the vehicle could be restored to its former glory.[86] Unfortunately, with other projects taking priority for the nascent Steam Railway in the 1970s, the tram chassis was pushed to one side and effectively left to rust for decades. Apparently unloved and forgotten, with its absent bodywork largely rotted or destroyed, it seemed to many that the tram car would never run again.

All this was to change when, after forty years out of service, the IWSR launched an appeal towards the restoration of Car No 2 in 2012. In many ways this was to be a virtual 'new-build' project, albeit one based around the surviving chassis. To suit the operational requirements of the IWSR's Wootton to Smallbrook line the new Car No 2 will include a brand-new diesel engine capable of operating at line speed and handling the route's gradients, while a slightly increased floor height will meet current platform levels. Where possible any surviving parts from the original vehicle, including door handles, window droplights and light fittings, will either be incorporated into the new vehicle or used as patterns for new replacement parts. A totally new-build replica trailer car is also under construction to accompany the restored tramcar; unlike the 1930s originals, this is to incorporate a driving position and disabled access. At the time of writing (April 2019) work on the restored chassis of Car No 2, being carried out by contractors on the mainland, is well under way with fitting of the new bodywork already started. Trams may never return to Ryde Pier (unless the Ryde-Shanklin line should ever be converted to a tramway itself), but elsewhere on the Island the Ryde Pier tram will one day run again!

The restored chassis of Ryde Pier Tramway Motor Car No 2 is seen at Alan Keef Limited in early 2019, with construction of the new bodywork already under way. *Alan Keef Limited*

From British Rail to Ryde Rail

For the remainder of the 'Rail Blue' era (from the early 1970s until the mid-1980s) it would be easy to think that not much happened on the Ryde to Shanklin line. Save for a few infrastructure changes, most of which might best be described as cutbacks and cost-saving measures, the Island's railway in the early 1980s might appear to have been little changed from that of the late 1960s. However, it was not expected to be this way. The Standard Stock trains had only ever been envisaged as a short-term solution, with a likely expected lifespan of about ten years. For this reason it seemed at the beginning of the 1970s that there were only two possible outcomes for the immediate future: either the trains would be replaced or the line would close altogether, depending on how full or empty your glass was. In the event neither of these things happened, and the Standard Stock would remain in service throughout the 1970s and '80s. Ultimately it was the events that *didn't* happen that perhaps most clearly defined this period.

Vectrail

The first event that failed to materialise in the 1970s was the planned revival of the Cowes-Newport-Ryde line by the Sadler-Vectrail company. The proposed formation of a group to take over the Newport to Cowes line following closure was first mentioned in the *County Press* in October 1965.[87] This group was to become the Vectrail Society, which by 1966 was hoping to lease the trackbed from Cowes to Smallbrook Junction from the Isle of Wight County Council, which was in turn negotiating with BR to purchase the freehold. A decision had also been made to operate the line using lightweight single-car diesel vehicles supplied by the Sadler Rail Coach Company of Southampton, reported *The Railway Magazine*.[88] The prototype vehicle then on test on the closed Meon Valley line in Hampshire had a maximum speed of 58mph and was capable of holding 50-75 seats, depending on spacing. In January 1967 the two organisations announced the formation of Sadler-Vectrail Limited, a new company dedicated to the acquisition and operation of the Cowes line. Six months later the prototype railcar made what would prove to be its sole visit to the Isle of Wight; it arrived on the 10.00am ferry at Fishbourne on 13 June for onward transportation to Ryde Airport, where it was displayed at the Island Industries Fair commencing on 21 June 1967.

A prototype Sadler railcar seen on test at Droxford, on the Meon Valley line, in 1966. If the Sadler-Vectrail project had been successful vehicles like this could have been operating on the Ryde-Cowes line in the 1970s. *F. E. J. Ward, IWSR Archive*

4-VEC No 046 approaches Sandown station with a northbound Shanklin-Ryde working in the early 1970s. A steam-era 'Whistle' board can be seen to the left of the train while on the right is a cast-iron Southern Railway warning notice. *Nick Doolan collection*

By the end of 1969 all indications were that the Vectrail project was heading for success. A Light Railway Order had been applied for and the County Council had formally agreed to lease the line to Sadler-Vectrail, the purchase of the line from BR having been almost concluded. Sadler-Vectrail itself was growing in confidence; having offered to take over operation of the Ryde Pier Tramway in 1969, by April 1970 the company was also planning a possible takeover of the Ryde-Shanklin line. As reported by the *County Press*, this proposal related to a rumour 'believed to have emanated from an authoritative source' that BR was planning to close the recently modernised line in December 1972. This 'golden opportunity' would include the likely replacement of the 'ancient former London Underground coaches', which Vectrail considered life-expired, although relaying the track from Shanklin to Ventnor would be out of the question owing to the 'astronomical cost'.[89] Meanwhile the Wight Locomotive Society, then based at Newport station, had also reached an agreement with Vectrail 'to operate its preserved stock on the line and to have its centre at Haven Street'.[90] Increasingly it seemed that the future of the Island's railways lay with Vectrail.

Some Islanders were not convinced by Vectrail's plans. Writing to the *County Press* in April 1970, a self-signed 'Road User' noted, 'I doubt whether anyone has done an economic exercise for Island transport but I would hazard a guess that it would show that Vectrail does not have a hope of surviving commercially.'[91] Sadly on this occasion the pessimists were proved right. In September 1970 the *County Press* reported:

'The Vectrail Society have abandoned their proposals to reopen the Cowes-Ryde railway as a modern commercial transport system.'[92]

A breakdown in the endless three-way negotiations between Vectrail, the County Council and British Rail was seemingly cited as the final straw at Vectrail's Extraordinary General Meeting, although *Wight Report* noted that 'the fate of Vectrail had in fact been decided some weeks earlier, when the chief investor withdrew from the enterprise.' Thankfully

the preservationists had anticipated these events: 'the failure of Vectrail has been expected for some time among the WLS Committee, and for this reason what has come to be known as the Haven Street Scheme has been prepared.'[93] Essentially this meant that the WLS would now become the master of its own destiny, purchasing the Havenstreet-Wootton section direct, while leasing the Havenstreet-Smallbrook section from the County Council to allow for possible future expansion. But what of non-heritage railway operations on the Isle of Wight? In March 1970 the Chairman of Vectrail had said, 'There are only two potential railway operators on this Island – British Rail and Vectrail'[94]; with Vectrail gone there was only one. The fate of the Cowes-Ryde section was sealed, but how much longer could Ryde-Shanklin survive?

Closure fears

The precise source of Vectrail's rumour that the Ryde-Shanklin line was to close in 1972 is unclear, but there is no doubt that closure fears were rife in the early 1970s. BR had axed around 47 miles of track on the Isle of Wight over the preceding two decades, so for the remaining 8½ miles to follow must have seemed almost inevitable. In 1966 a BR spokesman had only been able to guarantee the future of the line until 1975.[95] Conveniently the elderly Standard Stock units had been deemed to have about ten years of life left in them at the time of introduction to the Island, so would in theory be due for withdrawal in the mid-1970s. Opponents of the 1967 electrification had always argued that BR had spent too much money and done too little in a deliberate attempt to run down the Island's railways while simultaneously making them look as uneconomic as possible. The future was not looking rosy.

By January 1970 the Ryde-Shanklin line was reported to be running at a loss of £130,000 per year.[96] That same month *The Railway Magazine* noted that 'Conductor-guards commenced working on trains on the Isle of Wight on November 30, from which date ticket offices were closed for the winter at all island stations between Ryde St Johns Road and Shanklin inclusive.'[97] Ryde St John's Road, Sandown and Shanklin were to close their ticket offices again in subsequent winters, while Brading would remain permanently unstaffed from this point onward, its station buildings soon being

Set No 043 heads down Ryde Pier with a pier shuttle service in July 1978. Note that the first three cars, headed by 1928-built No S19, are in the blue-with-grey-doors livery introduced in 1976 while the final vehicle remains in original all-over blue. The abandoned pier tramway can be seen in the foreground. *Martyn Hilbert*

threatened with demolition. This proposed 'rationalising' of Brading was pronounced 'wasteful' by *Wight Report* 'in view of the serious financial position in which the Island railway must now find itself.'[98] Finally, in January 1972 the troubled line was granted a temporary reprieve when the Minister for the Environment announced a two-year grant of £204,000. The demolition work at Brading had still not been carried out although *Wight Report*, while welcoming the news of the grant, warned that 'the more settled future of the Shanklin line, together with its financial boost, may well result in the removal of existing buildings in due course.'[99]

The future was gradually starting to look more secure for the railway, but still doubts lingered on well into the 1970s. In 1973 the Isle of Wight County Council Roads Committee heard that the loss of the line within the next few years was 'pretty well on the cards'[100] while two years later the Isle of Wight Licensed Hotels & Establishments Association felt that 'the outlook for the future of the railway in the Island was not too rosy'.[101] Finally in 1976 the Southern Region's South Western Division Manager attended a meeting with the Island's councils at Newport to point out that any decision to close the line would be made by the Government, not BR, but that since the earlier closures the need to retain uneconomic services on social grounds had been recognised by the Government: 'The final decision is not ours to make because it is central Government which meets the deficit and which must be assured that a continuing railway represents value for money in terms of social need.' In other words it was now up to the local authorities to lobby the Government if they wanted the Island's railway to remain open on social grounds (which arguably is exactly what had already happened in the 1960s). Encouragingly he added:

> 'It is the wish of British Rail to see the Island railway retained and modernised in the belief that it still has a useful function – albeit a rather more limited one – than in the past.'[102]

Gradually the closure rumours receded and the Ryde-Shanklin line, like its ageing tube trains, carried on through the 1970s and into the 1980s.

Ryde Pier shuttle

As mentioned in the previous chapter, the Ryde Pier Tramway had been substituted by a 'shuttle service' of trains that worked from Ryde Pier Head to Esplanade before continuing empty to Ryde St John's Road to regain the up line and shuttle back in the opposite direction. The knock-on effect of this was that the peak service south of Ryde was reduced from five trains per hour to four, rendering the former up platform at Shanklin largely redundant as it became possible to concentrate all trains on the old down platform. In 1971 *Wight Report* noted that demolition of the up-side buildings had commenced on 9 August, while the subway had been filled in with rubble.[103] The loop on the up line was now used mainly for winter storage of rolling stock, and the signal box was only infrequently required. At the northern end of the line the existence of the shuttle would soon allow further economies to be made.

In October 1973 single-line working was temporarily introduced on Ryde Pier, all services being concentrated on the up line, after the scissors crossover at the mouth of the Pier Head station was found to be worn out. At first a new crossover was ordered but it quickly became apparent that savings could be made if the old crossover was simply replaced with two straight tracks and a new trailing crossover, controlled by Ryde St John's box, installed to the south of Ryde Esplanade instead. This had the added advantage of rendering the Pier Head signal box, which was itself worn out, redundant. The replacement scissors crossover, which had already been constructed on the mainland, was sold to the Bluebell Railway, which installed it at Sheffield Park, and the new arrangement at Ryde came into operation in May 1974.

From this point on the former up and down lines on the pier became two separate single lines with no physical connection above the new pointwork to the south of Ryde Esplanade. Services from Shanklin would, as before, travel via the (now bi-directional) former up platform at Ryde Esplanade, but could now only access the single-sided westernmost platform at Ryde Pier Head. Returning south the same train would travel back through the former up

4-VEC No 044 enters Ryde Esplanade station with a northbound working in May 1975. The Esplanade station was in the midst of a transition at this time; the newly constructed bus station can be seen on the left while on the right Platform 2 still retains its canopy. Both platform canopies are still in green and cream livery. *Gordon Edgar*

platform at Ryde Esplanade before regaining the down line via the trailing crossover as it approached Ryde Tunnel. This had the effect of freeing up the former down line on the pier, including the former down platform at Ryde Esplanade, for the exclusive use of the shuttle service, with trains free to shuttle up and down all day without the need to run empty to Ryde St John's Road. Unfortunately this meant that at the Pier Head the double-sided track serving Platforms 1 and 2, heralded in the 1960s for ease of loading/unloading, was now limited to shuttle services only, while the previously peak-service-only Platform 3 became the platform for all services going south of the Esplanade.

As described by *Modern Tramway* in the 1980s:

'…the east track on the pier became, in effect, an unsignalled tramway… It quite often happens that the shuttle and Shanklin trains race or chase each other along the pier, which to those not in the know must seem a funny way to run a railway.'[104]

The redundant Pier Head signal box, which had only narrowly avoided demolition by the MV *Shanklin* in 1973, was formally abolished on 5 May 1974 and subsequently removed.

Stations

In 1973 Mrs Irene Coates, Isle of Wight representative of the Conservation Society, wrote to the Southern Region General Manager to complain of BR's 'total neglect for many years' of the Island's stations. As reported by the *County Press*, Mrs Coates's letter was a damning indictment of BR's lack of investment at the time:

'They were wearing the old cream and green paint, grass was growing on the platforms and there was a large hole in Sandown station platform roof.'[105]

In fact, one of the Island's stations had received a 1st Prize in the Southern Region's Best Kept Station awards in 1971. Ironically this was Newport, on the closed Ryde-Cowes line, which still technically remained open at the time as a Parcels Concentration Depot. (With the tube trains having no parcels capacity, BR had transferred all of its Island parcels traffic to road transport after the end of steam, hence the parcels depot had no need to be rail connected.) According to *Wight Report*, the publicity surrounding the award had led to Newport being 'mentioned in the national press as the "station without trains"'.[106] Closure was announced a few months later and took place on 1 May 1972, when a new parcels depot was opened in the former Guards' Room at Ryde St John's Road station, the guards being moved to a new hut on the platform. Newport station was demolished in December 1972 while the parcels depot remained at St John's until abolished by BR in 1981.

In early 1972 *Wight Report* revealed that Ryde Council had given its approval to 'the rebuilding of Ryde Esplanade Station to incorporate a bus station'.[107] Work was begun in 1973 and included a new booking office and parcels office at the north end of the station. Three years later the buildings and canopy on the former up platform were finally repainted, while the canopy and buildings on the former down platform, not painted at the same time, were demolished in 1978 to be replaced with a fairly basic waiting shelter. At Sandown the buildings and canopy of the up platform were demolished in 1976, leaving behind only the very tall signal box, which had been designed to allow the signalman a clear view over the former canopy.

Shanklin station was further rationalised in 1979 with the removal of the former headshunt at the south end of the station to allow the demolition of the road bridge over Landguard Manor Road – something that had been predicted by *Wight Report* as long ago as 1971.[108] Reported the *County Press* in 1979:

'After the closure of this section of railway in 1966, the bridge formed part of a turning loop for trains at Shanklin station, but modernisation and more efficient working arrangements at the station has now rendered this manoeuvre unnecessary.'[109]

In reality 'modernisation and more efficient working arrangements' just meant fewer trains; the peak summer Saturday service was reduced to only three trains per hour in 1979, making the loop in the former up platform completely redundant. A new buffer stop was installed on the north side of Landguard Manor Road and the remaining platform (the former down platform) was extended at the northern end so that seven-car trains could still be accommodated after the southern end, which had extended out over the road bridge, had been demolished. With the loop removed, the signal box also became redundant and was demolished in 1980; the remains of Platform 2 were ultimately landscaped to form a flowerbed. From this point onward it became impossible for more than one train at a time to be south of Sandown. For road users and pedestrians alike the demolition of the old railway bridge removed a serious hazard; at only 12 feet across, it had only been wide enough for a single lane of traffic and no pavement. For the railway it marked a final severing of the route towards Ventnor.

With the down platform canopy at Ryde St John's Road reduced in length in the early years of electrification, and the eastern canopy at Ryde Pier Head removed during the 1980s, it was ultimately only Brading, threatened with demolition at the start of the 1970s, which survived completely intact. In fact, the unstaffed station was so untouched that by the mid-1980s it was heralded as the last station on the entire BR network still lit by gas lamps.

With the up platform canopy still intact, green and cream paintwork and Southern Railway signage, only the third-rail gives away the fact that this view of Sandown station was taken as late as 5 August 1976 and not decades earlier. Shortly afterwards the canopy and associated buildings on the up platform would be demolished, leaving only the signal box, which would survive until 1989. *Nick Doolan collection*

3-TIS unit No 033 leads a seven-car VEC-TIS formation into Brading with a southbound service on 25 July 1978. Note that the 1920s Southern Railway running-in board was still present even at this late date. The white stripes on the concrete posts are a wartime blackout measure, while the enamel sign was presumably installed by BR after closure of the Bembridge branch in the 1950s; the original SR sign advised passengers that they could change here for St Helens and Bembridge. *Martyn Hilbert*

Withdrawals and reformations

The earliest Standard Stock car to be withdrawn was DM No S15S, which was damaged in a shunting accident at Ryde Works in the autumn of 1967, just months after the electric service had been introduced. Since this left the Island with no spare car and repair would have been time-consuming, the decision was taken to purchase one more of the Standard Stock cars still stored by London Underground. The original No S15S was scrapped in May 1969 and the replacement car, also numbered S15S, arrived on the Island in 1971. Uniquely, the replacement No S15S was painted in BR blue livery at London Transport's Acton Works, the original forty-three cars having been painted by BR at Stewarts Lane. Three other cars, Nos S22S, S46S and S49S, damaged during transfer to the Island in 1966/67, were repaired at Ryde Works, but the purchase of the new S15S was the only occasion on which a replacement vehicle was acquired from LU, and would be the last tube carriage shipped to the Isle of

Wight until 1989. From now on the Standard Stock fleet would only get smaller.

A further shunting incident at Ryde St John's Road saw three cars withdrawn after 3-TIS No 035 and 4-VEC No 045 collided in 1973. The damaged cars were scrapped in 1974, while the remaining four vehicles were combined to form a new set, No 045. This meant that the Island fleet now consisted of one less three-car unit than in 1967, but with service levels reduced since the 1960s this would not prove a problem. A fire in 1975 led to the withdrawal of DM No S25S from 4-VEC No 046, with the surviving three cars becoming a spare three-car set with no driving position at the Shanklin end.

Car No S25S, the south-facing DM of 4-VEC No 046, became one of the earliest Island-based Standard Stock vehicles to be withdrawn, following fire damage in 1975. Not cut up until 1982, the unfortunate vehicle is seen here at the rear of Ryde Works in July 1978. To the left one of the former PMV vans, originally brought to the Island in the 1950s to carry passenger luggage, is in use as a store. *Martyn Hilbert*

3-TIS No 031, in all-over blue livery, heads a seven-car VEC-TIS formation as it arrives at Ryde St John's Road as a down working on 5 August 1976. At least fifteen tube cars can be seen in this image alone – more than the entire 21st century fleet. *Nick Doolan collection*

Another view from 5 August 1976, this time taken from the footbridge at Brading as 4-VEC No 041 arrives at the head of the 13.30 Shanklin to Ryde Pier Head service, formed of a seven-car VEC-TIS formation. *Nick Doolan collection*

In 1982 two cars from set No 033 were withdrawn to become stores vehicles, leaving just thirty-seven vehicles from the original forty-three-strong fleet still in service; this now consisted of five 4-VEC and five 3-TIS sets, together with one spare DM and one trailer. A shake-up in 1985 saw four more vehicles withdrawn and the remaining cars formed into five 5-VEC units and two 2-TIS sets, together with four spare trailers. From now on five-car trains became the norm between Ryde and Shanklin, something that would have been impossible with the original four- and three-car formations.

In 1982 3-TIS No 033 was disbanded, its trailer becoming a spare car and its DM being exchanged with one from 4-VEC No 043, while its Control Trailer was withdrawn and placed in the yard at Ryde Depot, where it remained in use as a store until broken up in July 1987. Built by the Metropolitan Carriage & Wagon Co in 1925, car No S30 is seen here on 21 June 1986. *Martyn Hilbert*

The disbanding of unit No 033 also saw the withdrawal of DM No S19, originally from 4-VEC No 043. Repainted dark green, the vehicle was placed in the former Platform 3 at Sandown where it too became a store, replacing two ex-Southern Railway PMV Utility Vans. Renumbered into the Internal User series in 1985 as 083569, the vehicle is seen here on 21 June 1986. Noted by *Rail* magazine in 1987 to be 'now grounded', the former S19 remained at Sandown until scrapped in 1989. *Martyn Hilbert*

No replacement trains

By the end of the 1970s questions were being asked about the continued suitability of the Island's tube trains. In 1978 a *Guardian* columnist recorded that the rolling stock 'makes the whole think (sic) look like something from an Ealing Studios comedy'[110], while in 1979 the Isle of Wight Licensed Hotels & Establishments Association described them as 'Cinderella's coaches' that 'gave visitors an unfortunate first impression'.[111] That the Standard Stock cars were showing their age was hardly surprising; they had after all never been expected to last this long in service on the Island. Many were now more than 50 years old and all had been considered life-expired by London Transport when originally withdrawn in the 1960s. By the mid-1970s London Underground was already withdrawing some of its 1938 Stock, but this was rejected by BR at the time on the grounds that the underfloor electrical equipment would be incompatible with operation over the sea when travelling up Ryde Pier. (Since the Standard Stock had been the final tube stock to feature above-floor switch compartments, this supposed problem would obviously apply to any tube stock built after 1938 as well.) With no apparent replacements in sight it seemed that the Standard Stock was there to stay.

The Island's tube trains have had few occasions to carry headboards. One exception was on 15 May 1983 when 3-TIS No 032 was at the head of the Isle of Wight portion of the Southern Electric Group's 'Submarine' rail tour from Clapham Junction to Shanklin. The remains of Platform 2 can be seen on the left. *Nigel Menzies*

In this well-known postcard view of Ryde Pier in the early 1980s, a seven-car VEC-TIS formation in all-over blue with grey doors is working the pier shuttle while another such unit can be seen at Pier Head station as a Shanklin service. Ryde Esplanade's Platform 2 can be glimpsed at the bottom left of the photo. The Sealink ferry at the Pier Head is one of the three Southern Railway-designed vessels launched in 1948-51 that monopolised the Portsmouth-Ryde run from 1969 until the mid-1980s. For a generation growing up in the 1970s and '80s it was these boats and trains that were the gateway to the Isle of Wight. *Author's collection*

3-TIS No 035 pulls out of Ryde Pier Head Platform 3 at the head of a seven-car VEC-TIS formation, the 11.10 service to Shanklin on 9 July 1983. Platform 3 would be renumbered Platform 1 later in the 1980s, and by the 21st century would become the only platform still in use. *R. S. Freeman*

Derailment

On 23 February 1981 three carriages of 4-VEC unit No 043 became derailed at Brading while forming the 22.12 Shanklin-Ryde service. Only two passengers were on board and both were unharmed, continuing their journey by taxi. The incident was particularly embarrassing for BR since it occurred only hours after a spokesperson had advised the *Portsmouth Evening News* that there was 'no likelihood' of the Island fleet being replaced in the foreseeable future:

'It was true, she said, that the 1938 stock would have been the most suitable, but even if British Rail had the money to buy the units, the newer carriages would not be available because they were still required by London Transport.'

This statement in turn had followed criticism from the Island's MP, Stephen Ross, that the existing trains were 'decrepit' and shook 'the daylights out of the passengers'.[112] Two years later the management at Ryde thought they had a solution to the problem of their ageing fleet.

The Class 503 proposal

On 25 April 1983 BR's Island Manager sent a report (reproduced in the Appendix to this book) to the Area Manager, Portsmouth, drawing attention to a recent 'marked increase in failures in traffic … which is causing widespread concern about the poor condition of the present Isle of Wight rolling stock.' Trains were being taken out of service on an almost daily basis with electrical or mechanical faults: sliding doors did not work properly, and rainwater was entering the driving cabs and passenger saloons through ill-fitting windows – which in turn was rotting the woodwork, upholstery and floors. Staff at Ryde were 'doing their best in difficult circumstances' but the increased failure rate was also creating a backlog in carriage cleaning.

Also included in the report is the perhaps surprising recommendation that 'the Class 503 electric units at present in use on the Wirral lines of the Liverpool Division … would be ideally suited to the Isle of Wight.'

In the 1960s BR had implied that second-hand tube trains were the only available stock that would fit the Isle of Wight's restricted loading gauge. At only 11ft 5in high, the Class 503s were lower than most mainland stock, having been built to serve in the tunnels of the Merseyrail network, but they were still around 2 feet higher than a deep-level tube train – so had BR been entirely truthful in the 1960s? The short answer is 'yes'. The Class 503s had not been available in the 1960s, being still required on Merseyside, and the Ryde-Shanklin line undoubtedly does have restricted clearances.

Famously, the main obstacle is the height clearance within Ryde Tunnel, which had been only 13ft 6in even before it was reduced further to 12ft 3½in during the winter of 1966/67. Less well known is the fact that the reverse curves within the tunnel also place restrictions on the length of vehicles permitted, while height restrictions also apply to certain other overbridges. On the other hand, it is worth stating that Ryde Tunnel is not a tube tunnel. The rolling stock that operated the line during the steam era, while somewhat elderly and diminutive, had not been designed with any restricted loading gauge in mind. BR's decision to raise the tunnel floor in the 1960s was only taken after it had been decided to employ tube trains, and even after that the diesel shunters that worked through the tunnel on maintenance trains continued to be considerably higher than the tube stock, even if some of them required cut-down cabs. In view of the fact that BR had first considered bringing tube trains to the Island at a time when it was contemplating closing all lines south of Ryde Esplanade (in which case the clearances in Ryde Tunnel might not have been an issue) it may be that the true appeal of the Standard Stock in the 1960s had been at least in part due to the fact that it was cheap and available, rather than just its size.

So, would a Class 503 fit the Isle of Wight's loading gauge? As can be seen in the accompanying photograph, a loading gauge test was conducted in the spring of 1983 when a wooden template, cut to the roof profile of a Class 503, was attached to the north-facing cab of a Standard Stock DM. Although not referred to in any of the paperwork, this was a local initiative that is understood to have likely taken place during April 1983, and most probably prior to the report dated 25 April (in which case the report was written as a result of the test, rather than the other way around). The roof profile was fitted at Ryde St John's Road and the train was able to successfully demonstrate adequate clearance along the whole Ryde-Shanklin line, including Ryde Tunnel, the only 'pinch points' being experienced at Smallbrook Lane Bridge on the down line and the up platform canopy at Ryde St John's Road. (Remarkably, the author has also been advised that 'should it have ever been necessary in the future' it was also determined that a Class 503 would have had adequate clearance through Ventnor Tunnel!)

The gauging test had proved that the profile of a Class 503 would fit the Isle of Wight loading gauge, but the length of the vehicles was another matter. The Driving Motor of a Class 503 was 58½ feet long

(the trailers were slightly shorter), while the Island's Standard Stock cars, although varying slightly in length between different designs, averaged around 51 feet. It was believed that this increased length would present a problem for trains passing through the sharp curves of Ryde Tunnel, so the report of 25 April proposed singling the track through the tunnel (this would not have been an option in the 1960s, when peak service frequencies still required most of the line to be double-tracked, but by 1983 this was no longer an issue). To achieve this it was proposed to remove the up line and slew the down line into the centre of the single-bore, double-track section that forms much of the tunnel's length. At the north and south entrances, where the tunnel consists of two single-track bores, the track could be lowered (presumably to pre-1967 levels) 'either by excavation or the use of slab paved track'. Other suggested structural alterations included raising the height of the platforms at Ryde Pier Head and Ryde Esplanade, while an extension to No 3 road at Ryde Depot would allow a three-car Class 503 unit to be serviced undercover without the need for additional shunting. (This was something that was not then possible for the Standard Stock cars, which were all formed into three- or four-car sets, while the depot was only two cars long.)

This rare photo shows the gauging trial undertaken circa April 1983. As can be seen, the train, fitted with a wooden template in the shape of the roof profile of a Class 503, is exhibiting no obvious clearance issues as it stands on the down line in the north portal of Ryde Tunnel. *Nigel Brodrick collection*

This wonderfully atmospheric shot shows DM No S4 from 4-VEC No 044 inside Ryde Works on 7 July 1984. The difficulties of handling three- and four-car units in a depot only two cars long is well illustrated. Note also that car No S4 is still in all-over blue with grey doors, while the vehicle on the adjacent track is in full blue/grey livery. *Bruce Galloway*

The view looking north from Ryde Esplanade station records the occasion of a particularly stormy high tide in the early 1980s, showing the waves crashing up between the tracks on the railway pier. This particular storm was the worst for several years, causing considerable damage to the eastern platform at Ryde Esplanade, while the pier head was inaccessible to trains and ferries for several hours. With conditions such as this it is easy to see why train services over the pier are at the mercy of both tides and weather. *Nigel Brodrick collection*

Also at Ryde, servicing of the underfloor-mounted equipment of the Class 503s would require alterations to the inspection pit facilities within the depot. Underfloor equipment was of course the very reason that the 1938 Stock had been rejected for the Island in the 1970s, on the grounds that it was thought to be incompatible with operation over Ryde Pier. This was no longer considered to be a problem, partly because the Class 503s were higher off the ground than tube stock but also because services over the pier were in any case withdrawn during exceptionally high seas, which occurred approximately three times a year. In fact, the report notes, 'it is short circuiting of the traction current, not damage to the rolling stock, that necessitates suspension of services.'

Why Class 503s?

But why the Class 503s in particular? In addition to their reduced height (and the fact that the Island Manager was already familiar with the units, being a regular visitor to the Wirral area) a key advantage of the 503s in 1983 was their availability. During 1984-85 the transfer of Class 508 units to Merseyside was to make the ageing Class 503s redundant, and thus potentially available for transfer elsewhere. By comparison it was thought likely that no suitable tube replacements would be available until around 1990. Many other advantages were also noted.

The Class 503s were built for operation on 650V DC third-rail so, unlike tube stock, would not need to be converted from fourth-rail operation. They had greater capacity than the Standard Stock cars, meaning that only twenty-seven vehicles, formed into nine three-car units, would be required. This would mean a 27% reduction in the number of vehicles required overall, and only nine DMs required instead of the present total of sixteen. All services could then be operated by either three- or six-car trains, meaning savings in both traction current and vehicle maintenance. 'Some services on Ryde Pier could be withdrawn' (possibly a reference to the Ryde Pier Shuttle.) The end of seven-car train operation would allow the shortening of platforms at Ryde Pier Head and Esplanade (where the timber platform ends were in need of replacement) and 'would also give a reduction in the construction costs of the proposed station at Lake'. The provision of guards' vans, absent from the Standard Stock, would also allow space for the carriage of bicycles, luggage and parcels, thereby generating extra revenue.

A handwritten memo, shown to the author, reveals that by 11 May 1983 a visit had been made to inspect the stock at Birkenhead and that a list of twelve three-car units had been drawn up from which the nine units wanted by the Isle of Wight should be selected. All of the vehicles shortlisted were from the batch of Class 503s built in 1956,

One of the Class 503 vehicles considered for possible Isle of Wight service was No M28374M, seen here at West Kirby in the spring of 1983. This particular vehicle did not make the shortlist compiled on 11 May 1983. *Nigel Brodrick collection*

rather than the earlier examples built by the LMS in 1938. Further positive assessments were made; the stock was well maintained with no visible signs of corrosion, and spare parts were in ample supply. The stock was said to be similar in design to a 4-EPB unit with a cab similar to a 4-SUB. The ride quality was also similar to a 4-SUB: 'a little noisy in tunnels but superior in every way to the I.O.W. units.' A six-car formation would provide 362 seats against only 236 in a seven-car VEC-TIS formation. Each coach carried forty advertising panels 'similar in principle to the LT system' (but surprisingly absent from the Island's Standard Stock), which was suggested as a possible source of extra revenue. Gangway connections could easily be fitted if required and it was also thought that the vehicles could be adapted for driver-only operation. Given their apparent condition, 'It should not be difficult to maintain the 503s on the Island for the next 25 years.' (That would have taken them until about 2010 – although given the propensity of Isle of Wight rolling stock to outlast its expected lifespan, one wonders if they would still be there now!) Signing off, the writer noted, 'I would recommend that we make a bid for this stock as quickly as possible.'

The Class 503 was clearly a good fit (in all senses of the word) for the Isle of Wight. So why was the proposal not followed through? In the end it seems likely that the problem was financial. The units themselves would not cost anything since, unlike London Underground vehicles, they were already owned by BR. However, there would still be costs incurred in refurbishing and shipping them to the Island, to say nothing of the infrastructure modifications mentioned in the report of 25 April. That same report also mentioned the 'strong possibility' that the Isle of Wight County Council might be prepared to contribute to these infrastructure costs, something that was underlined in greater detail in a follow-up memo sent on 14 May 1983. (The memo also mentions that the County Council had already written to the management at Waterloo regarding possible use of Class 503s on the Island.[113]) Perhaps this hoped-for contribution was not forthcoming? Or maybe BR already had a replacement fleet of tube trains in mind? The Island Manager was subsequently told that spending money on the necessary infrastructure adjustments could not be justified, and the Class 503 fleet was scrapped in 1985.

Livery changes

With their original 'Rail Blue' livery having remained unchanged for around ten years, in 1976 cars began to be outshopped from Ryde Works with grey-painted passenger doors. Non-passenger doors remained blue, except for the drivers' doors on the DMs, which continued to be included in the wraparound yellow cab ends. From the point of view of the 21st century, passenger doors painted in a contrasting colour to the rest of the bodywork is the norm throughout the rail network, being a requirement of accessibility regulations, but in 1976 this must have been quite a radical step. No other trains on BR were painted in such a way at the time, and probably none of the tube trains then operating on London Underground either. (Ironically today, forty years later, the Isle of Wight's current tube trains are virtually the only coaches in regular passenger service on the national network not to have a contrasting door colour, the application of a 'heritage' livery apparently allowing them immunity from accessibility regulations.) The 'S' suffix was dropped from the carriage numbers at this time.

Facelift

The entire fleet had received grey doors by the end of 1980, but further changes were to follow just two years later when the *County Press* announced: 'The Island's ageing rolling stock of railway carriages are being given a new lease of life with an £80,000 facelift.'[114] Part-funded by the County Council, which was understandably concerned about the impression tourists were receiving when first arriving at the Pier Head, this was to include a full refurbishment of both the interior and exterior of the tube cars. Internally the cars were to be repainted and fitted with orange linoleum floors, replacing the original slatted wood, and new moquette on the seats. (The moquette in question would have been familiar to some tourists as that used on London Underground's District Line D Stock trains since introduction in 1980.) Externally the tube cars were to receive full BR blue and grey livery (blue lower bodyside and grey around the window areas). Once again eyebrows must have been raised, as this was technically considered 'InterCity' livery at the time – although over the next few years the same livery was rolled out across BR's entire mainland suburban and rural fleets before sectorisation liveries began to take hold in the late 1980s.

Unlike most mainland fleets the blue/grey livery did not extend over the passenger doors, which remained in all-over grey, and the upper grey bodyside area did not extend much beyond the window areas. On the DMs this meant that the front third of the vehicle, where the above-floor switch compartment was housed, remained in all-over blue. Also introduced at the same time was the branding 'Isle of Wight' in large Rail Alphabet type ahead of the leading passenger doors on the DMs; this was the first time that Isle of Wight vehicles had carried prominent 'local' branding since being absorbed by the Southern Railway in 1923. The BR double-arrow logo was now moved from the cabside to be placed alongside the 'Isle of Wight' branding. An unusual feature of this was that the double-arrow was always placed furthest from the passenger door and nearest to the cab, meaning that on a north-facing DM the logo would precede the 'Isle of Wight' brand on the western side of the car but be placed after the brand on the eastern side (and vice versa on a south-facing DM). 'Correct' BR practice would normally have been to always place the logo before a brand and never after it.

As part of the new blue/grey livery, cab windows on the DMs began to receive black window surrounds – including a large black area below the shallow right-hand

4-VEC No 485042, led by DM No S22, arrives into Brading at the head of the 11.21 Shanklin to Ryde Pier Head service on 7 July 1984. The 'Ryde Rail' brand is still one year away, but the train is in the full blue/grey livery with the 'Isle of Wight' branding launched in 1982 and described as 'the distinctive Isle of Wight livery' in the Class 503 proposal. Brading station had long been unstaffed but someone has taken the time to install hanging baskets along the platforms. *Bruce Galloway*

An unidentified DM is seen inside Ryde Works on 15 May 1983 in the process of being repainted into blue/grey livery. *Nigel Menzies*

The interior of one of the cars from 4-VEC No 485041 was photographed at Ryde Pier Head on 21 March 1987. The moquette on the seats is that of London Underground's D Stock, introduced to the Island as part of the refurbishment programme begun in 1982, although this car appears to have retained its original slatted wood floor rather than the linoleum replacement. The yellow-painted area is that occupied by the guard. *Chris Lemon*

window to give the impression from a distance that both windows were of equal depth. Unit numbers, displayed as six-digit numbers incorporating the three-digit class number prefix for the first time, were now often displayed in this black area – previously the three-digit set numbers had generally been displayed at the top of the cab centre door. In 1983 the remaining Control Trailers were downgraded to trailers, losing their yellow ends in the process, so it is unlikely that any of them had received the black window surrounds by this time.

Oldest carriage

In January 1984 trailer No S43 received some special one-off branding after it was deemed to be the oldest passenger carriage still in service on British Rail. A mere sixty-years-young (positively youthful compared to the tube cars currently in service on the Ryde-Shanklin line at the time of writing!), No S43 had entered service on the Hampstead & City Line on 28 January 1924 and accordingly received the legend '1924 – 1984' on its lower bodyside (with a large double-arrow logo taking the place of the hyphen). That BR thought it appropriate to publicise the fact that it was still operating sixty-year-old carriages is in itself interesting – particularly when one considers that the rest of the Ryde allocation probably constituted the next thirty-six oldest carriages in service!

This metal pin badge is believed to have been designed for the 'Ryde Rail Festival' – an Open Day held at Ryde Works on 21 June 1986. The original artwork was drawn by Martin Heys. *Author's collection*

Ryde Rail

In the early 1980s the application of local route brandings was still something of a novelty on the BR network, but in 1985 the Standard Stock cars received a second local branding with the addition of the words 'Ryde Rail' to the DMs. With the 'Isle of Wight' lettering already carried ahead of the leading passenger doors, the new brand was now applied at the other side of the doors – so that the full branding now read 'Isle of Wight Ryde Rail' (or 'Ryde Rail Isle of Wight', depending on which side of the train you were looking at). Between the words 'Ryde' and 'Rail' was a large white silhouette of the Isle of Wight itself.

At the same time as the Ryde Rail brand was being rolled out a programme was begun to plate over the centre cab doors, which had long been a source of draughts in the cab. Cars so treated lost their centre window, having a plain flat panel up the middle of the cab, and here a large black silhouette of the Island was often placed, with the words 'Ryde' and 'Rail' respectively above and below it in small type. On these vehicles the six-digit unit number was placed across the top of the centre panel in roughly the same position that the old three-digit numbers had originally been placed at the top of the old cab doors. Three DMs were still in all-over 'Rail Blue' livery (together with grey doors) at this time, and at least one of them, No S4, received the 'Isle of Wight Ryde Rail' branding on its sides while still in the old livery.

Why Ryde Rail?

The origins of the 'Ryde Rail' brand are unclear, but it does on the face of it seem a rather idiosyncratic name to choose. For a start, the Island trains were already carrying a route brand, 'Isle of Wight', and in any case why choose *Ryde* Rail? Obviously like

Photographed on a southbound working at Ryde Esplanade on 11 April 1987, unit No 485043 displays to good effect the front-end treatment of a unit in full 1985-style 'Ryde Rail' livery. The plating over the centre cab door can clearly be seen. *Tim Brown*

An unidentified unit in 'Ryde Rail' livery faces up the pier as it waits at Ryde Esplanade station in September 1987. The central door pillar was not present on most Isle of Wight Standard Stock cars and identifies this vehicle as one of the DMs built no later than 1928. *Ron Fisher*

the Merseyrail brand (first coined in 1969) and Scotrail (1983) it was a regional variation on British Rail, but why not 'Wight Rail' or 'Island Rail' – or even 'Island Line'? Maybe it was just a pun on *Ride* Rail. Admittedly three of the then six stations on the line were physically in Ryde (and had Ryde in their name) and the Ryde end of the line – or at least the section of it on the pier – saw the bulk of the traffic. Nonetheless, for many passengers Ryde was just somewhere you travelled through en route to somewhere else; for Islanders it was a route to and from the mainland, while for the tourists who still compromised the greater part of the traffic it was a gateway to places elsewhere on the Island. Ryde is certainly a resort in its own right, but it was arguably the resorts at the southern end of the line that had saved the Ryde-Shanklin line from closure in the 1960s.

The 1980s were of course the era in which many BR depots started to customise their locos with their own unofficial emblems – for example Stratford's 'cockney sparrow' and Eastfield's 'Scottie dog'. The name did receive some official sanction (at least during the Network SouthEast era), but it may well be that 'Ryde Rail' and the accompanying Isle of Wight silhouette were simply Ryde Works' own attempt at customising its fleet. Whatever the reason, there is no doubt that 'Ryde Rail' had a certain ring to it. It was a memorable brand and one that is still fondly remembered today by enthusiasts of a certain age.

The name Ryde Rail continued in regular use until the end of the decade – and lingered on for as long as there were still Standard Stock cars on the Island – but even in 1985 it was soon to be subsumed within a much more dominant brand. British Rail was transforming the way it managed its network and a new forward-thinking business sector was set to take over BR's passenger operations within the south-east of England. The red lamp posts of Network SouthEast were coming.

The Diesel Shunters

5

Freight and parcels traffic may have been abolished on the Ryde-Shanklin line at the end of 1966 but, for the next three decades, one or more locomotives would still be required for the operation of engineering trains. As a result the Isle of Wight became notable not only for its tube trains but also as a last bastion for types of diesel shunter that had become extinct elsewhere on the national network.

'Nuclear Fred'

On 15 October 1966 the *Isle of Wight County Press* reported on the arrival of

> '... a diesel shunter on the Fishbourne car ferry. The locomotive, mounted on a low loader, was formerly in use at Parkestone Quay near Harwich and is to be used on the Island for service work, ballasting, etc, after electrification of the railway.'[115]

This locomotive was No D2554, a 1955-built Hunslet 0-6-0 diesel shunter (later Class 05) that had been transferred from the Eastern Region in July 1966 and located at Fratton until finally shipped to the Island on 7 October. Some accounts state that the locomotive visited Eastleigh Works during its sojourn at Fratton to have its cab height reduced, although in fact this does not appear to have been necessary. No D2554 was one of the original batch of Class 05s (Nos D2550-D2573), which, as built, had a cab height of only 11 feet, so should have been easily compatible with the reduced 12ft 3½in height of Ryde Tunnel after 1966/67.[116] (Arguably the low cab height may explain why this particular type of loco was chosen for Isle of Wight service in the first place.) According to *The Railway Magazine*, 'Drivers from the Isle of Wight had been training on No D2554 at Fratton.'[117]

No D2554 was the first ever diesel locomotive to work on the Isle of Wight and the first 'new' railway locomotive of any description to be shipped to the Island since the last of the 'O2s' had arrived in 1949. It would also be the last BR loco shipped to the Island until its replacement arrived in the 1980s. At the time No D2554 was the youngest loco, by about half a century, to have worked on the Island; despite this it still wore the old British Railways green livery complete with lion-and-wheel crest, as opposed to the new 'corporate image' blue livery applied to the tube vehicles that were arriving around the same time. In accordance with long-standing steam-age tradition, the locomotive was positioned with its cab towards Ryde Pier Head and its bonnet facing towards Shanklin. The same policy would be adopted for its successors when they arrived in the 1980s.

On arrival at Ryde No D2554 soon earned the nickname 'Nuclear Fred', apparently due to the clouds of smoke emitted when it was started up after a period of non-use. In April 1967 the loco was photographed with this name displayed on an attractive, and not insubstantial, unofficial nameplate carried on the locomotive's bonnet in the manner of a headboard, although how long the name was carried is uncertain. Two observers of the Island's railway scene in the 1960s can recall seeing the loco 'always carrying her nameplate' when parked in the bay platform at Sandown over a period of time, possibly as long as several months, during 1967 – yet another contemporary has advised the author that he never once witnessed the nameplate in situ, despite regularly seeing the loco at Ryde St John's Road during the same period and specifically looking out for the nameplate. (Although see the image at the top of page 62 for evidence that the shunter did make at least one appearance at Ryde St John's with its nameplate in place). Given these apparently contradictory reports one has to wonder if the unofficial headboard-like addition was actually being taken on-and-off the loco on a regular basis. Certainly photographs show No D2554 to have been unnamed in March 1967, and nameless again later in the 1960s. Regardless of the status of its nameplate, the nickname remained in use throughout the loco's time at Ryde, although frequently it was referred to simply as 'the diesel' – it was after all the only one.

On 29 December 1966, just two days before the end of steam, the recently arrived No D2554 can be seen keeping company with its predecessors in the steam shed at Ryde St John's Road. Next to it stands No W22 *Brading* and in front of it No W27 *Merstone. R. Tibbits, Colour-Rail.com*

In March 1967, still not carrying its 'Nuclear Fred' nameplate, No D2554 heads south from Ryde Esplanade station on an electrification works train. Much work seems to be in progress on the northbound platform – not surprising, as the line was due to reopen later that month. *Colour-Rail.com*

By April 1967 the Island's shunter had finally received its short-lived 'Nuclear Fred' nameplate, as evidenced by this photo taken at Ryde St John's Road. Many early shots of No D2554 show it carrying a single white headcode disc – the steam-era headcode for the Ryde-Ventnor line. *T. E. Hastings, IWSR Archive*

could in any case only be undertaken with the aid of a match wagon. With the introduction by British Rail of the TOPS computer system in the late 1960s the locomotive was classified as a Class 05 – by the end of 1968 it was the *only* Class 05 left on British Rail as all its sisters had been withdrawn during the previous two years. A few examples lived on in industrial use, some of which have since been preserved.

In January 1972 No 2554 (BR had dropped the 'D' prefix from its diesel locomotives after the end of steam) was finally reliveried to match the tube trains, becoming the only Class 05 to carry Rail Blue livery whilst in BR service. *Wight Report* noted that 'Ryde have made a good job of repainting, for which the engine was long overdue.'[118] Another first was clocked up two years later when the loco became the only member of its class to carry a TOPS number, becoming No 05001 in 1974. By this time it was no longer the only diesel on the Island, the Isle of Wight Steam Railway having taken delivery of its first shunter in June 1972.

One final renumbering was to follow in 1981 when the erstwhile 'Nuclear Fred' was transferred to Departmental stock, becoming No 97803 in the process. By now its days were numbered. The Class 503 proposal document[119] details not only the poor reliability of Standard Stock vehicles in the first quarter of 1983 but also the sorry performance of the Island's solitary diesel shunter during April of that year, recording that, after having failed twice in two weeks, the loco was taken for a test run on 22 April. At this point it was again declared a failure 'until further notice', leading to the cancellation of a driver training course scheduled to begin on 3 May 1983 – a training course that had already been delayed 'due to earlier failure of locomotive'. One year later a replacement loco arrived on the Island, the Class 05 being withdrawn due to a faulty gearbox.

Over the winter of 1966/67 'Fred' was put to work on the electrification preparations, most notably on the rebuilding of the railway pier at Ryde. In 1948 the newly nationalised British Railways had inherited twenty-seven Isle of Wight-based locomotives from the Southern Railway; the withdrawal of the final two 'O2s', Nos W24 *Calbourne* and W31 *Chale*, in March 1967 would leave No D2554 as the sole remaining BR locomotive on the Island. Indeed, for the next few years it and *Calbourne* (the latter thankfully preserved by the Wight Locomotive Society) would represent the only two locomotives of any type on the Isle of Wight.

With electrification completed in March 1967 No D2554 seems to have led a fairly pedestrian life with few excursions onto the main line. With its use on the main line only permitted when the track was under an Engineer's possession, the loco was usually to be found in daylight hours parked in the Engineer's sidings at Sandown, or sometimes at Ryde Works. Forays up the pier, or trips down to Shanklin, were definitely the exception rather than the norm. Shunting the tube carriages was not a regular role as 'Nuclear Fred' was vacuum-braked only and coupling

First repainted blue in January 1972, No D2554 was renumbered into the TOPS series as 05001 in 1974. In this view taken at Sandown in July 1978 the loco is seemingly fresh from another repaint and is yet to have its full number reapplied – appearing instead as '0500'. *Martyn Hilbert*

Following the electrification works of 1966/67 the Island's Class 05 was usually seen parked in the sidings at either Sandown or Ryde St John's Road. Rarely moving in the hours of daylight, it and its successors had little reason ever to venture as far north as Ryde Pier. Nonetheless, as this rare photo shows, the former 'Nuclear Fred' did make at least one final trip up the pier after being renumbered into the Departmental fleet as 97803 in 1981. The precise date is unknown but must be some time prior to withdrawal in 1984. Engineering works appear to be in progress in the vicinity of the Pier Head platforms. *Neil Higson*

One year before its withdrawal, No 97803 is seen sandwiched between two Standard Stock cars at Ryde St John's Road on 15 May 1983. The difference in height between the shunter and the tube cars is easily appreciated. *Nigel Menzies*

Happily the withdrawn 'Nuclear Fred' was bought by the IWSR, the *County Press* reporting on 31 August 1984 that the shunter had been 'transported from St John's Station at Ryde by low loader during the week' – arriving at Havenstreet in time for display at the annual bank holiday Steam Extravaganza.[120] Appropriately this would see it reunited with No W24 *Calbourne*, the two locos having both been employed on electrification works during the early months of 1967.

At Havenstreet the Class 05 quickly regained its pre-TOPS number D2554 and before long was repainted into BR green livery for the first time since 1972. Today the locomotive is categorised by the IWSR as part of its 'heritage fleet' (the only non-steam loco on the IWSR to be regarded as such) although the lack of air brakes means that it is unable to haul passenger trains, being instead confined to the occasional shunting duty. Refurbished mechanically and cosmetically in recent years, No D2554 can usually be found on display within the IWSR's 'Train Story' building, once more proudly carrying the name 'Nuclear Fred' on its bonnet.

The Class 03s

The replacement for 'Nuclear Fred' was Class 03 No 03079, which was carried to the Island by the Sealink car ferry *St Helen* on 8 April 1984, having spent the previous month based at Eastleigh for crew training duties. Built at Doncaster in 1960, the vacuum-brake-only locomotive was only five years younger than its predecessor but was nonetheless welcomed by the *County Press*, which noted that BR would now be able to 'catch up on a 12-month backlog of track maintenance and relaying', while a BR spokesman stated that the new arrival was 'an indication of an assured security for the Shanklin line in the foreseeable future.'[121] On transfer to the Island the Class 03 was also transferred to the Departmental fleet, being officially renumbered as 97805 – although in practice it continued to carry the number 03079.

With a cab height of more than 12 feet the Class 03 was considerably higher than its predecessor, but, surprisingly, remained on the Island for several months before its cab was reduced. What happened during this period is even more surprising. A former senior member of staff recalls a nocturnal test run in circa August 1984 during which No 03079 headed north from Ryde St John's Road on what was, in effect, a somewhat secretive mission to confirm that it would pass through Ryde Tunnel. 'The reason for

this test was to try and get 03079 into service as quickly as possible… It also provided one last opportunity to demonstrate that a Class 503 would pass through Ryde Tunnel, although this subsequently fell upon deaf ears.' Working wrong line over the down line, the unmodified loco was eased through Rink Road Bridge, which is notably lower than the tunnel itself, before successfully passing through the entire length of the tunnel, 'although it was found to be rather tight in places'. From there the loco crossed over the points south of Ryde Esplanade and proceeded to work up the western track of the pier, making possibly the only known appearance of a Class 03 at Ryde Pier Head station.

Heading back south *down* the up line, the 03 successfully traversed the tunnel again before almost getting stuck under Rink Road Bridge, where up line clearances were known to be tighter than on the down line (in fact, the up-line clearance at Rink Road is nominally slightly lower than the roof of an unmodified Class 03). From here the loco was taken back north to Ryde Esplanade before regaining the down line and making one final journey through the tunnel, successfully clearing Rink Road Bridge on the down line, and retiring hurt to Ryde Works with only minor damage to the cab roof. One month later, in September 1984, the cab was rebuilt at Ryde with a slightly lower roof profile, in a manner similar to the cut-down cabs of the Class 03s used on the Burry Port & Gwendraeth Valley Line.

On the mainland the earliest withdrawals of Class 03s had occurred as long ago as 1968; nonetheless they were still well represented on most BR regions, although notably absent from the Southern when 03079 was shipped to the Island in 1984. Four years later in 1988 the once 230-strong class was down to single figures on BR when *Motive Power Monthly* reported the surprising news that 'The Isle of Wight is to receive a 200% increase in working

Class 03 No 03079 is seen inside Ryde Works in September 1984 in the midst of having its cab height reduced after its unfortunate encounter with Rink Road Bridge. The cab roof, which has been temporarily removed, can be seen on the floor in front of the loco. *Mark Brinton*

One year after arriving on the Island, the reduced-height No 03079 is captured outside Ryde Works during an Open Day on 9 July 1985. Behind it can be seen Standard Stock DM No S5 in Ryde Rail livery. *Gordon Edgar*

No 03079 gives brake-van rides to members of the public at Sandown on 21 June 1986, the day of the 'Ryde Rail Festival'. The brake-van is ex-Southern Railway 15-ton 'Pillbox' Goods Brake Van No DS55724, since preserved at the Isle of Wight Steam Railway. *Martyn Hilbert*

representatives of this class on the Island.' One of these was destined for the Isle of Wight Steam Railway (reported at the time as No 03089, although it would eventually be No 03059 that was purchased) to assist with track-laying on its planned extension to Smallbrook Junction as the one-time 'Nuclear Fred' was 'not sufficiently reliable for this work'[122]. More surprising, however, was the news that dual-braked No 03179, officially withdrawn from Ipswich in 1987 but since employed by the Engineer's Department, was coming to join the similarly numbered 03079 on the Ryde-Shanklin line to assist with the singling of the double-track section between Brading and Sandown. Ironically the redundant track would be donated to the IWSR for the construction of its Smallbrook extension, meaning that the rails that No 03179 would be helping to lift in one location were the very same rails that No 03059 would be helping to relay elsewhere. At the time it was (incorrectly) reported that once the track-lifting was complete No 03079 would be withdrawn and become a source of spares for its replacement, No 03179. In reality, however, it was new arrival No 03179 that was intended to be a strategic spare, to be kept in service at Ryde but with only minimal maintenance undertaken. For the first time since 1967 Ryde would have more than one locomotive in its fleet.

The choice of No 03179 for transfer to the Isle of Wight had been made after an emissary from Ryde visited several mainland locations to examine stored Class 03s with a view to selecting a suitable candidate. All of the stored locos were found to be in poor condition, many of them vandalised, leaving only the two still in regular service – No 03179 at Ipswich and No 03059 at Colchester – as practical choices. Colchester was apparently unwilling to part with its loco, having recently repainted it in BR green for an Open Day, so No 03179 was selected for Ryde. That No 03059 would also end up on the Isle of Wight, albeit at Havenstreet rather than Ryde, just months after No 03179 is of little coincidence; a contact at Ryde had made the IWSR aware of its suitability.

Having been shipped to the Island on Sealink's *St Cecilia* on 30 June 1988, no time was lost in reducing No 03179's cab height, with a correspondent for *Rail* magazine spotting the cab-less loco mid-conversion at Ryde Works on 19 August.[123] Less expected was the news that the loco was also to receive full Network SouthEast (NSE) livery, with the repainted shunter, photographed in December 1988, becoming the magazine's February 1989 cover star. Elsewhere in the same issue, Nos 03179 and 03079 – the latter newly outshopped in Rail Blue – were pictured side by side at Ryde, the magazine noting: 'It is likely these two shunters will not regularly be seen together as 03179 will be at Ryde with No 03079 at Sandown.'[124] Ryde Works had done a surprisingly impressive job of translating the full NSE 'toothpaste' colour scheme to the diminutive loco, with the addition of red coupling rods and black funnel and air-tanks. With the class soon to be extinct on the mainland, No 03179 would be the only Class 03 ever to carry NSE livery. Meanwhile,

with the Standard Stock soon to be phased out, No 03079 would become the last Rail Blue vehicle on the Ryde-Shanklin line.

But if No 03179 was the 'spare' loco, why was it chosen to receive such an extravagant livery treatment while sister No 03079 was repainted in the altogether more humdrum Rail Blue colour scheme? The answer is surprisingly mundane. With all tube stock repaints now being carried out in NSE colours, Ryde had little use for Rail Blue paint and at the time of No 03179's repaint, carried out under the pretext that it had to be painted in order to protect it, the depot staff believed that they had run out of the old colour. Subsequently a further tin of Rail Blue was discovered by one of the fitters, so the opportunity was then taken to use up the old stock by repainting No 03079 in blue.

In February 1989 a change in BR policies saw the two Island 03s transferred from Departmental stock back into capital stock, although in practice this made no difference to the locos whatsoever; No 03179 had never been allocated a Departmental number, and No 03079 had never carried its official number of 97805. The transfer did temporarily boost the number of remaining 03s in capital stock to five, although the following month would see the last three mainland examples withdrawn, leaving No 03079 and '179 as the final survivors. Once again the Isle of Wight had become the final outpost for a class of loco extinct elsewhere on BR. A further administrative move in 1990 saw the two shunters nominally transferred to Eastleigh, prompting *Motive Power Monthly* to dryly comment: 'The two locomotives will, of course, remain on the Isle of Wight.' Both were described as 'normally kept at Sandown'[125]. In fact, both Class 03s appear to have carried 'RY' depot stickers (RY being the TOPS code for Ryde) throughout their time on the Island – surely not strictly necessary on an isolated network with only one depot?

It is tempting to wonder how two diesel shunters managed to find gainful employment on the 8½-mile line, particularly when one locomotive had been enough during the years 1967-88. So it probably came as no surprise when 'spare' NSE-liveried No 03179, out of use for some time, was officially withdrawn on 29 October 1993. Blue-liveried No 03079 lingered on for three more years, probably the last vacuum-brake-only locomotive on BR, before its own official withdrawal on 3 June 1996. In reality, noted *Rail* magazine, it had 'been out service for over two years'[126]. No 03079 was now laid up at Sandown while No 03179 remained at Ryde. A few months later *Rail* reported: 'Both are expected to pass into preservation during 1997.'[127] For No 03079 this was to prove correct, but for No 03179 events were about to take an unexpected turn.

On 31 May 1998 No 03179 is reported to have made one final trip onto the main line[128], travelling under its own power from Ryde St John's Road, where it had been stored since its withdrawal in 1993, to Sandown, where its withdrawn sister No 03079 remained. Five days later, on 5 June, both locomotives were transferred to low-loaders and left the Island for the last time. No 03079 was destined

No 03179 remained at Hornsey until sold in 2016 to the Rushden, Higham & Wellingborough Railway.

When the two Class 03s departed from the Isle of Wight in June 1998 the Ryde-Shanklin line was left without a diesel shunter for the first time since 1967. With track maintenance duties taken over by road-rail vehicles, which could be easily transported to the Island as and

for the Derwent Valley Light Railway, where it remains to this day; No 03179, however, was returning to use on the national network. In August 1998 *The Railway Magazine* reported that 'No 03179 has been acquired from Island Line by West Anglia Great Northern Railway for use at Hornsey depot.'[129] For several years No 03079 had held the distinction of being the last Class 03 in use on the national network; this remarkable turn of events would now see No 03179, originally withdrawn on the mainland as long ago as 1987, take that title. At the north London depot the loco acquired the nickname 'Clive' and, continuing its penchant for colourful one-off liveries, lost its NSE colours first to receive WAGN and later First Capital Connect livery (surely making it the only shunter to receive either of these colour-schemes?). Finally withdrawn, for the third time, in 2008,

when required, their usefulness was over. The Island Line had bid farewell to its final locomotives. Except…

Of course, Nos 03079 and 03179 had been only two of three Class 03s on the Isle of Wight – No D2059 (aka 03059) remained at Havenstreet on the Steam Railway. Four years after the two Class 03s had departed from the Island, the sight and sound of a Class 03 returned to the Ryde-Shanklin line when No D2059 was hired by the privatised Island Line, together with two ballast hoppers, to operate ballast trains over the weekend of 16-18 March 2002. *Island Rail News* (the successor to *Wight Report*) reported: 'D2059 behaved impeccably throughout the operation, as did the hopper wagons.'[130] Owing to there being no rail connection between the Island lines at Smallbrook Junction, No D2059 was instead delivered to

Over the weekend of 16-18 March 2002 the Isle of Wight Steam Railway's Class 03 No D2059 was hired together with two ex-London Transport ballast hoppers to operate ballast trains over the by then privatised Island Line. Pictured here in Brickfields siding, Sandown, this remains the only occasion on which preserved vehicles have ever operated over Island Line metals. *L. Pullinger, IWSR Archive*

Sandown by road. To date this is the only occasion on which the IWSR's Class 03 has visited the line, but the apparent ease with which the preserved loco was allowed to travel over what remains technically part of the national rail network must surely raise hopes that one day other preserved stock may yet be allowed to visit the line.

Preservation

As may be gathered, the Isle of Wight Steam Railway, although unashamedly a 'steam' railway, had nonetheless been acquiring a small fleet of diesel shunters ever since the arrival on loan of *Spitfire* in the 1970s had brought about the retirement of the former Ryde Pier Tramway chassis. An 0-4-0 shunter built by Ruston & Hornsby in 1946, *Spitfire* had in the 1960s been employed on the former Meon Valley line by the Sadler Rail Company, with the *County Press* noting in 1972 that it had once been 'earmarked for transfer to the Ryde-Cowes line, where it would have been put to use on shunting duties had the Sadler-Vectrail scheme succeeded.'[131] Ironically, though the scheme fell through, the loco was destined for the Isle of Wight anyway, arriving at Havenstreet on 5 June 1972. A late-1970s IWSR guidebook gives the loco's number as 39, following in the IWSR's then policy of continuing the pre-preservation Isle of Wight numbering sequence. (The highest numbered Island loco in pre-preservation days had been No W36 *Carisbrooke*, so the two tank engines imported by the steam railway in the 1970s, *Invincible* and *Ajax*, had been numbered 37 and 38 respectively.) Perhaps damning with faint praise, the guidebook notes, '*Spitfire* has proved invaluable (if spasmodic) service to the line.'[132]

On 3 October 1984 the Railway doubled its diesel allocation with the arrival of a 1954-built North British 0-4-0 donated by Esso Petroleum from Fawley Oil Refinery, which was subsequently named *Tiger* and painted in the one-time maroon livery of the Isle of Wight Railway. In 1984 *Tiger* was fitted with Westinghouse air brake equipment allowing it for the first time to operate with the Steam Railway's air-braked passenger stock (unlike on the mainland, the Isle of Wight's steam trains had long been air-braked rather than vacuum-braked). The first public outing for *Tiger* on passenger services appears to have taken place on Sunday 21 October 1984 when a car boot sale at Havenstreet included 'A Rare Opportunity to Ride on the Island's Only Diesel Hauled Train Service' for the princely sum of 60p per head.[133] That same year the Class 05 'Nuclear Fred' had arrived at Havenstreet, bringing the Steam Railway's diesel fleet to a total of three shunters.

As mentioned above, the IWSR acquired a BR Class 03 in 1988. This was the air-braked 1959-built No 03059, which arrived at Havenstreet on 4 November 1988, having sailed overnight on the 23.00 Portsmouth-Fishbourne car ferry. Previously based at Colchester, the loco was already something of a celebrity engine, having for some time carried the nickname 'Edward' and had been repainted in BR green livery complete with lion-and-wheel crest and its pre-TOPS number D2059. It would retain this livery for

some years at Havenstreet before being repainted in BR black in 1994. Reporting on the loco's arrival, *Rail* magazine noted that the low-loader that had brought No D2059 over to the Island had on its return trip 'moved unserviceable Ruston shunter *Spitfire* back to the mainland for its new home at the Northamptonshire Ironstone Railway.'[134]

The final changes to the IWSR's diesel fleet, to date, occurred in the early 1990s with *Tiger* departing for the Scottish Railway Preservation Society at Bo'ness in 1991, only to be replaced by 1945-built Andrew Barclay 0-4-0 shunter No 235, unofficially known as 'Mavis', which arrived on long-term loan from the National Army Museum in 1992. In 2008 the National Army Museum donated No 235, together with two Hunslet 'Austerity' Class steam locomotives, to the Steam Railway. Since the 1990s the IWSR's diesel fleet of three shunters has remained unchanged. Nos 235 'Mavis' and D2554 'Nuclear Fred' are primarily confined to shunting within station limits at Havenstreet, while Class 03 No D2059 'Edward' is the railway's 'Thunderbird' locomotive, called upon to work timetabled passenger trains in the event of a steam engine being unavailable and, in an emergency, able to rescue a failed steam train.

Diesel Galas

Over the weekend of Friday 30 September-Sunday 2 October 2016 the IWSR celebrated the 50th anniversary of the arrival of 'Nuclear Fred' on the Island by holding its first ever diesel gala. A two-train service was operated, with all passenger services hauled by either the railway's own Class 03 No D2059 or by visiting 03 No 03197 (not to be confused with the similarly numbered former Ryde resident No 03179). 'Nuclear Fred' itself operated brake-van rides at Havenstreet, while the ex-Army No 235 could be seen shunting wagons. One year later the Railway made the surprising move of shipping a Class 33 'Crompton', No 33202 *Dennis G. Robinson*, to the Island for its second diesel gala. This was the first ever main-line diesel to visit the Island and the largest locomotive of any type to cross the Solent; it also remains the largest ever load carried by a Wightlink ferry. Passenger trains were operated by Nos D2059 and 33202 (the latter mainly working between Havenstreet and Smallbrook, as it was too large to fit the headshunt at Wootton), while 'Nuclear Fred' once again operated brake-van rides at Havenstreet. Also displayed at Havenstreet was No 03197, which somehow still hadn't left since the previous year's gala.

Having returned to the mainland, 03197 was back again the following autumn for the Steam Railway's third diesel gala over the weekend of 28-30 September 2018. On this occasion the gala was dominated by Class 03s, with all passenger trains operated by Nos 03197, 03399 (also visiting) or D2059. For the first time since 1998 there were, temporarily, three Class 03s on the Isle of Wight.

The future of diesel shunters on the Isle of Wight Steam Railway seems to be assured. Whether diesel traction, in any form, will ever return to the Ryde-Shanklin line remains to be seen.

Looking immaculate after a recent overhaul, No D2254, the Isle of Wight's original diesel shunter, is seen on display in the Isle of Wight Steam Railway's 'Train Story' building on 21 June 2017 – reunited with its original 1960s 'Nuclear Fred' nameplate. *Andy Sansome*

The Network SouthEast Years

In the mid-1980s British Rail's management structure was reorganised with the creation of five business sectors: InterCity, Railfreight, Parcels, Provincial (later Regional Railways), and what was originally called the London & South East (L&SE) sector. Initially this latter sector, which included the Isle of Wight within its boundaries, made little public impact, with its so-called 'Jaffa Cake' livery only appearing on a handful of mainland multiple units until on 10 June 1986 the sector was very publicly relaunched as 'Network SouthEast' (NSE). On the Isle of Wight, as elsewhere, the rebranded sector would quickly make its mark with trains and stations repainted in its striking new colours of red, white and blue. Soon would follow new stations and a wholesale replacement of the Island's ageing tube trains in what would prove to be the biggest investment programme in the Ryde-Shanklin line since the electrification of the 1960s.

New livery

The application of NSE livery to the elderly Standard Stock cars was probably the first way in which the new sector really made its presence felt on the Isle of Wight. The first tube car to emerge in the new colours was Driving Motor No 9 (the 'S' prefix was dropped from the carriage numbers upon repainting), which entered Ryde Works for repainting at the end of January 1987 and was pictured in the May issue of *Motive Power Monthly* posing outside Ryde Works in its new livery on 11 February.[135] Surprisingly No 9 had only the previous year been painted in blue/grey – purportedly the final Standard Stock car to receive that livery as well as the first to be unveiled in NSE colours.

As applied to the Standard Stock, the livery was a fairly faithful interpretation of the original version of NSE livery – albeit with the proportions adjusted to suit the dimensions of a tube train. The only obvious difference

The first Standard Stock car to enter service in Network SouthEast colours was DM No 9 (the 'S' prefix was dropped from the car numbers upon repainting). The recently repainted vehicle is seen here at Ryde St John's Road on 11 April 1987. *Tim Brown*

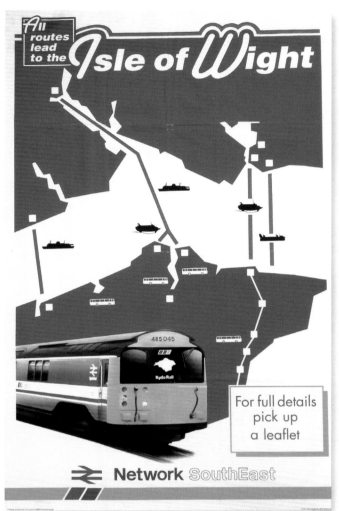

This late-1980s Network SouthEast poster promotes connections to the Isle of Wight. The fact that the focus of the poster is a reliveried Standard Stock unit – rather than any of the Island's tourist attractions – evidently shows that NSE was not ashamed of its elderly tube trains. *Author's collection*

from mainland practice was the lack of a diagonal upsweep at the end of the unit; the bands of blue, white, red and grey simply continued horizontally along the side of the cab instead. The yellow cab ends still wrapped round onto the side of the vehicle, but only now as far as the driver's door, the door itself no longer being yellow. The double-arrow logo returned to the cab-side with the words 'Ryde Rail' now appearing in small Rail Alphabet letters below the logo; as with most mainland stock, the 'Network SouthEast' logo was in larger type within the white band further along the driving vehicle. On the cab front itself the black window surrounds were extended across the plated-over central cab doors to form a large black rectangle across the front of the vehicle, in a similar manner to that employed on Railfreight-liveried Class 20s. (The application of large black areas around the cab window areas is common practice on the railways of the

21st century – ever more so now that yellow ends are being phased out – but in the 1980s, when black window frames were only just coming into vogue, it was still quite a striking move.) Within this black rectangle a white Isle of Wight silhouette was normally placed where the central cab window would once have been, with an NSE red/blue/grey flash above it and the words Ryde Rail below. Many photographs show DMs running without the Isle of Wight silhouette – maybe the transfers (if it was a transfer) were in short supply. Also in many instances the Ryde Rail name appears to have been condensed to a single word, 'RydeRail', on both the cab front and cab side, although this was certainly not the case on DM No 9.

That NSE livery was applied to such elderly vehicles so early in the life of the new sector is itself interesting and perhaps indicates the importance that NSE attached to its overseas outpost. On the mainland some of the Southern Region's less glamorous fleets were still being outshopped in blue/grey livery at this time.

By March 1987, according to *Rail Enthusiast* magazine, cars Nos 9, 10, 28 and 93 were all in the new livery, while Nos 34 and 94 were due to receive it shortly, as well as either No 11 or No 15. Four cars were still in all-over blue with grey doors while the rest of the fleet were in blue/grey. Six vehicles were due for withdrawal, with the remaining twenty-seven cars to be reformed into five five-car sets and one two-car set; the latter was intended to consist of one of the two aforementioned cars Nos 11 or 15, both of which were DMs (one would be repainted in NSE; the other would be withdrawn) coupled to Control Trailer No 28, which, uniquely, was having its driving controls reinstated.[136]

Control Trailer No 28

DM No 9 may have been the first Isle of Wight vehicle unveiled in NSE livery, but the first vehicle on which repainting actually got under way was CT No 28, with *Motive Power Monthly* (describing the situation at Ryde in January 1987) noting: 'This car is already repainted on one side only in NSE livery.'[137] All the surviving CTs had been downgraded to Trailer Cars in the early 1980s, with their cab equipment removed. The decision to return just one of them to use as a CT in the late 1980s would therefore make car No 28 unique – and certainly visually distinct from the other driving vehicles in use, all of which were DMs. As a CT, No 28 lacked the distinctive clerestory cab roof profile of the DMs and had two full-depth cab windows as opposed to the uneven windows of the DMs. It had also lost its original head and tail lights when the cab fittings had been removed and these were now replaced with a modern halogen light fitting quite unlike anything on the other vehicles. As if these differences weren't enough, on re-entry to service No 28 initially retained its central cab door, meaning it still had three windows across the front and did not receive the large black rectangle around the cab windows; in fact, it had no black window surrounds at all. The cab door was subsequently plated over and a black rectangle applied,

3-TIS No 486031, with CT No 28 at the rear, arrives at Brading with a southbound working on 7 January 1989. Platform 2 has been out of use for little more than two months – note that track is still in situ – and, with red canopy supports and NSE signage, looks rather better maintained than the derelict structure on Platform 1, which retains the peeling green and cream paintwork of the steam era. Just six months later the Platform 1 building would be restored and relaunched as a community centre. *Chris Lemon*

The by then unique Control Trailer No 28 is seen at Shanklin at the head of a northbound working circa 1989. By this time No 28 has acquired a sealed centre cab door and black window surround but is still instantly recognisable due to its non-clerestory roofline and modern light fittings. Note also that by this date Shanklin has acquired 'step-free' access from platform to train. *Author*

but the combination of modern headlight and unusual roof profile meant that No 28 remained easily identifiable to the end.

The same issue of *Motive Power Monthly* also noted the hope that at least one complete unit would be reliveried in time for the planned opening in May of a new station at Lake, midway between Sandown and Shanklin.

Lake station

That there was need for a seventh station on a stretch of line only 8½ miles long might seem surprising, but demand had been there for a very long time. In early February 1966 a meeting of the Lake Ratepayers' & Residents Association had debated the need for a station to accompany the forthcoming electrification works and had decided to recommend 'the end of Heath Road as a possible site of a halt'[138]. Almost exactly twenty-one years later, on 16 February 1987, Network SouthEast began construction of a small station at that very location, the ceremonial first sod being turned by Captain G. W. Buttle, County Councillor and life Vice-President of the very same Ratepayers' & Residents Association.

At the ceremony Captain Buttle recalled the events of two decades earlier and remarked that Lake had waited more than 80 years for a station, noting: 'Research has revealed that in 1904 there were plans for a halt.' In fact, Lake had been waiting even longer than that; the minute books of the old Isle of Wight Railway Company show that demands for a halt at Lake had first been made in the 1880s. In the 1960s the need to maintain peak-time service frequencies had made such a suggestion out of the question for BR, but by the 1980s a reduction to only three trains per hour had put Lake back on the agenda – as evidenced by the reference in the Class 503 proposal to 'the proposed station at Lake'[139].

That Captain Buttle was so supportive of the 1987 scheme is surprising as the Lake Ratepayers' & Residents Association itself was now actively campaigning *against* the County Council's grant of £30,000 towards the total cost of around £80,000, and had already written to the Council to say that 'Lake halt will only be an advantage to a small percentage of Lake residents.'[140] The Council itself had been only too willing to encourage the fact that 'for the first time in many years British Rail … gave the impression they are prepared to invest money in this line.'[141]

Situated approximately three-quarters of a mile south of Sandown, Lake was opened for traffic on Monday 11 May 1987 and proved an immediate success. Only a short walk from the beach, it was arguably better located for day-trippers than either Sandown or Shanklin. An official opening ceremony followed on 9 July 1987, at which it was revealed that around 300 people a day were now using the unmanned station, with BR's Island Manager announcing that 'on a recent Saturday 220 people used Lake in just two and a half hours'. Mr J. Ellis, the Southern Region's Deputy General Manager, was also present to reassure the gathered dignitaries that 'Lake station was

clear evidence that BR had no intention of closing the Ryde to Shanklin line.'[142] Located on the eastern side of the single-track line, the new station comprised a single wooden platform with a glazed shelter of the type favoured by NSE. Interestingly, the 110-metre-long platform had enough capacity for seven-car trains, despite the fact that almost all vehicles were now (officially) formed into five-car sets.

The opening of Lake was a momentous day for the Isle of Wight's railways, being the first new station to be built on the Island since the St Lawrence branch had been extended to Ventnor Town (later Ventnor West) in 1900. Remarkably, however, it was not the only station to open on the Island that month. On 31 May 1987 Chris Green, NSE's charismatic director, visited the Isle of Wight Steam Railway to formally open its new station at Wootton. While there he pledged 'every help to the steam railway in their proposed extension to Smallbrook Junction and an interchange with the Ryde Rail Ryde-Shanklin line.'[143] The success of the IWSR's extension would mean that Lake would not be the only station to be constructed on the Island by Network SouthEast.

Sandown-Brading singling

At the official opening of Lake, Mr J. Winkles, BR's Island Manager, had spoken of forthcoming economy measures that it was hoped would lead to savings of at least £50,000 a year. As reported by the *County Press*, 'the proposals would entail reducing the number of signal boxes which would mean the loss of some signalmen's jobs and reductions in the amount of track by two miles.'[144] Thankfully, this 2-mile reduction did not refer to a shortening of the line but rather to the singling of the double-track section between Brading and Sandown, thereby reversing an improvement introduced by the Southern Railway in the 1920s. The signal boxes to close were Sandown and Brading, which would both become redundant; with Ryde Pier Head and Shanklin boxes having been demolished in the 1970s, this would leave Ryde St John's Road signal box in sole charge of the line.

The work to single the track was carried out over the weekend of 29-30 October 1988, with the final train to call at the former down platform at Brading being the 21.07 Ryde-Shanklin service on Friday 28 October. Over the weekend tracks were severed and realigned, with the former down line now becoming the sole running line. Services over the new alignment were resumed on Monday 31 October. Both signal boxes officially closed on Saturday the 29th, although a cabling problem led to the temporary reopening of Sandown box until final closure on 25 February 1989; demolition following one year later. At Sandown the passing loop was retained, while at Brading the down track was removed (although, unusually, not the conductor rail, which was left in situ to assist with running rail return resistance[145]). This rendered not just the signal box but also the footbridge and former island platform out of use. As mentioned in the previous chapter, the redundant track panels were subsequently donated to the Isle of Wight Steam Railway for use in the construction of its extension to Smallbrook Junction.

In the short term the singling of the former double-track section was a practical decision. The days of five trains per hour had long since passed, and the retention of the loop at Sandown meant that the then regular service pattern of three trains per hour at 20-minute intervals could still be maintained. (The other passing point was the remaining double-track section between Ryde Esplanade and Smallbrook Junction). In the longer term this was to prove an unfortunate decision, as only a few years later the service was reduced to two trains per hour, which meant that, in the absence of a loop at Brading, services could only be operated at 20/40-minute intervals rather than a regular 30-minute interval. Since there have been no further track or pointwork changes since 1988, the Island has now been blighted with this irregular service pattern for a very long time.

'New' trains for old?

The NSE livery may have been modern, but by 1987 the remaining Standard Stock cars were looking positively ancient. With an average age of around sixty years, the tube trains had now been on the Island for twenty years – a decade longer than had been anticipated. The Class 503s had been ruled out, for whatever reason, and with new-build stock out of the question it seemed that the only possible replacements would be more second-hand tube trains.

In July 1987 a visiting journalist from *Rail* magazine was told that 'consideration was being give [sic] to obtaining 1962 LU stock when it becomes redundant in around 1990.'[146] One year later the same magazine wrote of 'increasing speculation' that 1938 Stock cars, the last of which had been retired by London Underground on 19 May 1988, might be supplied as short-term replacements as the hoped-for 1959/62 Stock was not now expected to become available 'until at least 1992'.[147] That same month *Motive Power Monthly* was confidently reporting that the replacement trains would be three-car sets of 1938 Stock, to be rewired and overhauled at Ryde before entering service. At the same time an NSE spokesman was quoted as saying that 'no final decision had yet been taken' while 'another

source' had suggested that BR was still planning to wait for the 1962 Stock to be cascaded from the Central Line 'in 1990/91'.[148]

Finally in August 1988 it was confirmed that some of the 1938 Stock was to be transferred to the Isle of Wight. These very same trains had been rejected fifteen years earlier on the grounds that their underfloor electrical equipment would be unsuitable for working over Ryde Pier; but, as the Class 503 proposal had pointed out, services over Ryde Pier were already suspended in the event of exceptional high seas.

As announced by the *County Press:*

'Network SouthEast will spend £900,000 on the scheme, fully refurbishing the fleet of eight two-coach trains which will come into service in May next year… Unlike the present trains, which operate in fixed five-coach formations, the new fleet will be more flexible allowing two or four coach trains to be run as demand requires.'[149]

In other words, the trains would operate in two-car units. The Class 503 proposal had suggested extending Ryde Works to accommodate three-car units; evidently BR had decided that a cheaper option would be to simply shorten the trains. In part this would be alleviated by the greater seating capacity of the 'new' trains – a result of the electrical equipment being located under the floor instead of occupying space behind the driver's cab, and the fact that this time around no seats would be removed to provide extra luggage space. Nonetheless, the new two- and four-car formations would be a far cry from the seven-car trains that had been in use only a few years previously. Reporting the announcement, *Rail* magazine commented: 'Although half a century old already, [the 1938 Stock] are in considerably better condition than the current vehicles,' and noted that 'whether any of the older stock will be retained remains to be seen.'[150] No further mention was made of the possibility of acquiring the much younger 1962 Stock.

Island Line

With the new stock was to come a new brand name, which has been associated with the Ryde-Shanklin line ever since. In August 1989 *Motive Power Monthly* carried a list of new localised brandings that Network SouthEast was rolling out across all of its routes 'to mark its third anniversary'[151]. Alongside existing NSE brands such as 'Thameslink' and pre-Grouping names like 'Great Northern' were many names now lost to history. Among the very few brands that would survive the forthcoming upheavals of the privatisation era was 'Island Line'.

But of course the Isle of Wight's trains already had a distinctive brand name. All of the Standard Stock units, whether in blue/grey or NSE livery,

A view inside the cab of one of the Driving Motors of No 485045, seen at Shanklin on 7 January 1989. *Chris Lemon*

One of the first prominent uses of the new 'Island Line' brand came in the form of these large banners, celebrating the launch of the 'new' 1938 Stock, prominently displayed at all stations in the summer of 1989. The pluralisation of 'trains' is somewhat premature, as only one two-car unit was actually on the Island when this banner was photographed at Sandown on 15 July – two days after the official launch. *Martyn Hilbert*

were emblazoned with the name 'Ryde Rail', and as recently as January 1988 *Rail* had reported that NSE had invested in new signage 'on 11 station platforms, incorporating the Ryde Rail logo'[152]. ('11 station platforms' might sound a lot for the Ryde-Shanklin line, until one remembers that at the time the majority of the original stations still retained two operational platform faces.) Why change the name? The reasons are unclear but, as previously pointed out, Ryde Rail was a slightly odd name for the route when well over half the track mileage wasn't actually in Ryde at all. Maybe someone at NSE thought the old name was just a little too idiosyncratic? 'Island line', in the singular, had been an accurate description of BR's Isle of Wight network ever since the closures of 1966 (the Ryde-Shanklin line was referred to as the 'Island line' in an issue of *Wight Report* as far back as 1968[153]). Whatever the reason, 'Island Line' was the name chosen to be rolled out alongside the 'new' trains in 1989. The new brand was never carried by the Standard Stock cars, which retained the Ryde Rail name until the end, but the 1938 Stock would be marketed as Island Line from the outset – remaining so throughout their Island career despite changes of ownership and livery.

(It is perhaps entertaining to ponder what other choices NSE might have considered. A simple 'Isle of Wight' brand, as carried on the Standard Stock cars from 1982 onwards, would have been as geographically straightforward as some other NSE brands – or maybe 'Isle of Wight Electrics' could have joined 'Wessex Electrics' and 'Anglia Electrics'? Alternatively, since the ferry company of the same name was not formed until 1990, could 'ThamesLink' and 'Kent Link' have been followed by 'Wight Link'?)

Introducing the 1938 stock

The 1938 Stock vehicles chosen by Network SouthEast for the Isle of Wight were all to be Driving Motor cars; no Trailer Cars were ordered, meaning that both vehicles in every two-car unit would be powered. Cars were to be transferred from London Transport's Ruislip depot to BR's Strawberry Hill, before onward movement to Eastleigh for overhaul.

Originally delivered to London Underground in the years 1939-40, the oldest vehicles were, somewhat embarrassingly only five years younger than some of the Standard Stock cars they were replacing. (This was actually an improvement on the situation in 1967, when the oldest of the newly introduced Standard Stock cars had been barely, if at all, younger than some of the steam-hauled stock they had replaced.) The irony that BR was to replace ancient tube trains with more ancient tube trains was not lost on the national press, with *The Guardian* drolly commenting:

'Network SouthEast has been slapping up posters, congratulating itself on the introduction of new rolling stock this year. The Isle of Wight is, at last, getting more modern units for the Ryde Pier-Shanklin line… Splendid. And what rolling stock is this, exactly? Strangely, the posters don't mention this point. It is, in fact, also former London Transport stuff (ex-Bakerloo Line). Dating from 1938.'[154]

At the end of 1988 hopes were running high that the Island's new trains, to become Class 483, would be in service quickly. 'The first seven coaches of the replacement LT 1938 stock were due to be shipped to the Island during December for entry into traffic early in 1989,' reported *Rail* magazine, noting that 'most of' the Standard Stock fleet was expected to be withdrawn in January. (On a happier note for the Standard Stock, 'Two coaches of the 1923 stock may be retained as a vintage train.' [155]) Just one month later the same magazine was reporting on concerns that 'the "new" Isle of Wight stock … will not be ready in time for the summer season.'[156]

Quickly it became clear that delivery of the 'new' units was falling behind schedule and the bulk of the remaining Standard Stock vehicles would have to soldier on for at least another twelve months. In the spring of 1989 ex-London Underground car No 11184, soon to become car No 221 of unit No 483001, was photographed at Eastleigh partially repainted in a trial version of NSE livery.[157] The units were to be numbered in the sequence 483001-

483008, with the 'A' ends numbered 121-128 and the 'D' ends 221-228.

The decision to reduce the 1938 Stock to two-car units may have enabled the trains to fit into the depot at Ryde, but it might have had other unintended consequences at the conversion stage. Nick Brown was working for the Railway Technical Centre at Derby at the time (the 1938 Stock conversion project was managed by an RTC office at King's Cross) and recalls a, possibly apocryphal, story that circulated on the office grapevine:

'When Unit 001 was tested before leaving works, the two vehicles tried to drive off in opposite directions. After a plaintive phone call from Eastleigh, one of our electrical engineers realised that when the '38 Stock was built, certain train wires crossed on one of the inter cars.'

Finally on 30 June the completed two-car unit undertook its first trial run on the mainland, working from Eastleigh to Winchester. Further test runs followed for No 483001, the final one taking place on 3 July, before the unit travelled from Eastleigh to Fratton, via Woking, on 4 July. That day the two cars were lifted from their bogies and transferred to lorries for onward transport to the Isle of Wight, which took place the following day; the

The first refurbished 1938 Stock unit outshopped from Eastleigh was No 483001. The still unnumbered unit is seen here at Eastleigh on the main line on 30 June 1989 – the day it undertook its very first test run to Winchester. Just one week later the same unit would be delivered to Ryde St John's Road. *Colour-Rail.com*

Only two weeks after being outshopped from Eastleigh, No 483001 stands in the shuttle bay at Ryde Pier Head from where it will form the special inaugural service of the 'new' Isle of Wight trains on 13 July 1989. Note that by this time the eastern canopy, which would have been on the left of the picture, has been demolished. The train is to call at both Smallbrook (to unveil a banner on the site of the future IWSR interchange) and Brading (for the opening of the new community centre on Platform 1). *BR(S) Official, IWSR Archive*

vehicles were reunited with their bogies upon being unloaded and rerailed at Sandown. On 6 July the new set finally arrived in Ryde Works, being hauled from Sandown by a five-car set of the old Standard Stock. Once again the DMs were positioned with the 'A' car facing toward Ryde and the 'D' car facing Shanklin. On returning to the mainland, the low-loaders carried back Standard Stock cars Nos 43 and 47, which were to be hauled to Strawberry Hill before, like so many redundant rail vehicles of the time, being disposed of by Vic Berry of Leicester.

Launch

Having originally hoped to have the whole fleet in service by the spring, Network SouthEast finally had one 1938 Stock unit on the Isle of Wight. A launch date had by now been set, so on 13 July 1989, just one week after leaving the mainland, unit No 483001 was officially launched into service with great ceremony. At Ryde Pier Head the unit broke through a banner reading 'Network SouthEast Welcomes New Isle of Wight Trains'. Helping to hold the banner was NSE Director Chris Green, who revealed that several Island stations were due to be upgraded within the next two years, saying, 'Let there be

Network SouthEast Director Chris Green addresses the invited guests at the launch of the 'new' trains at Ryde Pier Head on 13 July 1989. With No 483001 launched in the shuttle bay, and no other new trains yet on the Island, the train behind Mr Green in Platform 1 (formerly Platform 3) is, somewhat embarrassingly, one of the old Standard Stock units. *BR(S) Official, IWSR Archive*

Five days after its launch into service, No 483001 is seen parked in the sidings at Ryde St John's Road on 18 July 1989, to the left of No 485004. When not parked at St John's the 1938 Stock unit was at first largely restricted to Pier Shuttle duties – as indicated by its route indicator, which is displaying 'Pier Head-Ryde-Esplanade'. The contrast between the 'old' and 'new' trains is striking, although in reality DM No 7, at the centre of the picture, was less than a decade older than its replacements. *Martyn Hilbert*

Right: With their bogies removed, cars Nos 127 and 227, comprising unit No 007, are seen on low-loaders at Sealink's Gunwharf terminal, awaiting their sea voyage to the Isle of Wight. The photographer records this as being 13 March 1990, although most other accounts give the date as the 12th. *David Rowland*

Below: One of the changes needed at Ryde Works to accommodate the 1938 Stock was the construction of a new raised track to facilitate access to the underfloor equipment on the new vehicles. Unit No 007 is here seen on this new facility in May 1992. *A. Blackburn, IWSR Archive*

no doubt that we are committed to the Island routes – it is something British Rail is extremely proud of.'[158] With festivities at Ryde Pier Head dealt with, No 483001 carried its party of invited guests down the line, pausing first at the site of the former Smallbrook Junction for the unveiling of a large sign announcing a future interchange station with the extended IWSR, due to open there in 1991. After this the unit proceeded to Brading, where a further ceremony was to take place.

Brading

Having been threatened with demolition several times over the years, the entire station complex at Brading, including the footbridge, signal box and buildings on both platforms, had been formally listed by English Heritage in 1986 on the grounds that it was the most complete surviving station complex on the Isle of Wight. This would ensure the long-term survival of all of these structures, despite the fact that the singling of the line to Sandown in 1988 rendered most of them redundant. The launch into service of No 483001 on 13 July 1989 saw a double ceremony enacted at Brading: the signal box was formally handed over to the IWSR for relocation to its proposed new station at Smallbrook, while the long-disused building on the former up platform (by now the only platform still in use) was reopened as a heritage and community centre, a project described by the *County Press* as 'the largest of its kind undertaken by British Rail's community unit'. The Mayor of Brading, Mrs Marianne Sullivan, announced: 'A day that was hitherto a dream has now become a reality and a derelict and redundant railway station has become a centre to benefit the entire community.'[159]

In fact, the IWSR had originally hoped to acquire rather more than just Brading's signal box; the Winter 1988/89 edition of *Wight Report* announced the news that BR had agreed to hand over not only the signal box, but also 'the two waiting rooms and canopy from the Down side platform'. Noting the listed status of the station, the article stated that 'it's hoped an application for delisting will allow relocation of the redundant structures to the proposed Smallbrook interchange in due course.'[160] Evidently the hoped-for delisting was not forthcoming since it was only the signal box that would be formally handed over on 3 July 1988. (Given the platform layout that was constructed at Smallbrook, it is difficult to see how the Brading buildings and canopy would have been utilised anyway.) In the event, even the signal box would remain at Brading, boarded up, while the new community centre on Platform 1 would become neglected again after only a few years of use – but see Chapter Eight for more recent, happier, events at Brading.

'One previous careful owner'

Aside from the fact that only one train had actually been delivered so far, the unavoidable fact at the launch of the 'new' trains was that they were obviously not new at all. This was jokingly acknowledged by Chris Green when he informed the gathered dignitaries that the trains had had 'only one previous careful owner'[161]. What he probably didn't say was that, at fifty years of age, the 1938 Stock was actually around ten years *older* than the Standard Stock had been upon delivery to the Island in the 1960s.

Thankfully any closeness in age between the 1938 Stock and its direct predecessors was belied by its appearance. Where the clerestory-roofed Standard Stock cars had been clunky and angular, the 1938 Stock benefited from the smooth, clean lines of 1930s art deco modernism. These were tube trains of a different generation and they looked it. With their below-floor equipment, the 1938 Stock vehicles were arguably the first 'modern' tube trains; their design influencing future tube stock for decades to come. Even today there are tube trains running in London that might be said to share a family resemblance with their 1930s predecessors.

Livery

Aside from their 'modern' appearance, one factor that certainly helped to sell the 1938 Stock as 'new' trains was the quality of its interior and exterior refurbishment, and in particular its livery. As with the Standard Stock, Network SouthEast livery was applied, but this time it was the very latest version of the livery, with not only a darker shade of blue but also a light grey band in place of the dark grey of the original. The white band was now much narrower, although still wider than the red band and, unlike on the

Standard Stock, this time the diagonal upswing at the end of the units was included. The double-arrow logo was now absent, while the Network SouthEast logo appeared in the white band near the non-driving end of one car per unit, and a small Island Line branding appeared on the same alignment in the centre of both cars. On the front of the unit the cab windows had a black surround while the lower half of the cab was yellow with an NSE flash in the centre of the central cab door, which was not plated over. Pioneer unit No 483001 initially had a slight wrap-around of the yellow cab end while on later deliveries the grey from the side livery was extended to meet the black cab window frame.

In effect, this version of NSE livery, with the light grey band, was the livery that had debuted on the brand-new 'Wessex Electrics' units only the year before and would subsequently be applied to all new NSE units until privatisation; older mainland units continued to receive a modified version of the original dark grey band version. That the Island Line units were deemed worthy of this livery is undoubtedly an indication of NSE's faith in its 'new' trains.

At least one *County Press* reader had their own ideas, feeling that tourists were 'heartily sick of NSE' and that BR should instead recognise the tourist potential of its vintage rolling stock and 'paint the new stock in good old Southern green… In fact, if folk travel to see what is, in effect, a working museum, extra revenue would ensue.'[162] The Island's 1938 Stock would eventually receive a tourist livery – and a heritage livery – but not just yet.

Route indicators

Unlike on the Standard Stock, the three-line route indicators located below the right-hand cab window were not plated over and remained in use. This may seem unnecessary on a line where 'Ryde Pier Head' and 'Shanklin' might appear to be the only possible destinations, but in reality the fact that the pier shuttle was still in operation meant that 'Ryde Esplanade' was still a regular destination, while photos from the time show that the trains could also display combinations of 'Special', 'Not in Service', 'Ryde St John's', 'Brading' and (later) 'Smallbrook Junction'.

Entry into service

With one unit present for the official launch in July 1989, the delayed arrival of the rest of the fleet slowly began. The NSE spokesman who told *Motive Power Monthly* that 'The full fleet should be operating by the end of October'[163] proved somewhat optimistic, but nevertheless by the end of September the *County Press* was able to report: 'There are now six new coaches on the Island'[164] (in other words, three new trains). In addition to pioneer unit No 483001, these new units comprised Nos 483002, which had spent several days crew training at Fratton prior to transferring to the Island on 25 September, and 483003, which had departed from Eastleigh for Fratton on 26 September and thence to the Island the following day. As had happened with No 483001, all units continued to be sent from Fratton to Sandown on low-loaders that were then used to carry their Standard Stock predecessors back to the mainland for scrapping. Testing on the Island for Nos 483002 and 003 began respectively on 28 and 29 September 1989.[165]

With three units in service for the start of the 1989 winter timetable, the Island would have to wait until the spring before any further sets arrived. On 2 February 1990 units Nos 483004 and 005 began mainland testing on the Shepperton branch, where they clocked up reported speeds of 55mph[166] – the same two units went on to better this the following month when, en route to Fratton for transfer to the Island, they reached a reported 60mph on the down gradients of the Haslemere line.[167] (Nos 004 and 005 were not the only Island tube trains to record impressive speeds on the mainland in 1990; that autumn a five-car set of redundant Standard Stock vehicles – returning to London to form a proposed LU heritage set – would themselves reach 55mph on the journey up from Fratton.[168])

Nos 004 and 005 arrived on the Island on 14 and 15 March 1990, joining No 007, which had arrived on the 12th, to make up a trio of units delivered that month. The Isle of Wight now had six new units ready for the launch of the summer timetable in May 1990 – by which time the rapidly dwindling number of Standard Stock vehicles left in service could be counted in single figures. Early summer saw the eventual arrival of No 483006 on 20 June, its non-sequential arrival being seemingly explained by a need for repairs at Eastleigh earlier in the year[169], followed two days later by the intended final unit, No 483008. The introduction of the Isle of Wight's 'new' trains had officially been marked by the ceremonial launch of No 483001 on 13 July 1989; exactly one year later on 13 July 1990 No 483006 became the final unit of the original batch of eight trains to formally enter service.

Runaway train!

No sooner had it entered squadron service on the Isle of Wight than the 1938 Stock was making headline news – but unfortunately not for the right reasons. On Saturday 12 January 1991 the 17.14 service from Shanklin departed from the station while the train crew were still on the platform. One passenger later told the *County Press*: 'We closed the doors when it started moving quite fast and tried to stop it by pulling the communication cord but that did not work.'[170] Seemingly the train, a hybrid two-car unit consisting of cars Nos 123 (from 483003) and 224 (from 483004) had been left unmanned with the brake off while the driver changed ends and had simply rolled away down the gradient towards Sandown. Since it was freewheeling, neither the communication cord nor the dead man's handle appear to have been operational. Having passed through Lake without stopping, a quick-thinking passenger, who obviously knew what he was doing, managed to break into the empty cab before finally bringing the train to halt at Lake Hill Bridge by applying the emergency brake. Two weeks later the *County Press* reported that 'two independent inquiries' had ruled out any technical faults with the train and that BR had already taken action to prevent a repeat incident by adjusting the gradient at Shanklin.[171]

Units 483009 and 010

Surprisingly, units Nos 483006 and 008 were not the final 1938 Stock trains to arrive on the Isle of Wight. The number of withdrawn 1938 Stock vehicles transferred to Eastleigh in 1988-89 had been greater than the required fleet of sixteen vehicles, and eventually it was decided to convert two further cars. The resulting unit, No 483009, consisting of cars Nos 129 and 229, was delivered to Sandown on 9 April 1992. One day earlier had seen the arrival of two 'spare' vehicles, which were nominally allocated the set number 483010. Described by *Rail* magazine as 'replacement cars in the event that one of

The unused 'spare' set, No 010, uniquely painted in all-over NSE blue, is seen parked in the headshunt near Ryde St John's Road on 25 March 1993. On the left can be seen Standard Stock DM No 5 from the by then withdrawn Sandite unit formed of cars Nos 5, 31 and 28. *Andy Sansome*

the existing vehicles is withdrawn from traffic'[172], the spare cars were essentially just two empty shells that were in no way intended to form an operational unit. Largely stripped of fittings and with its windows boarded-up, No 010 was painted in a unique livery of all-over NSE blue, which, rather surprisingly in the circumstances, included yellow cab ends. In the event the spare cars were never required and for many years could be seen in the sidings at Ryde St John's Road, their blue paint slowly fading.

Ride quality

In 1988 Chris Green had promised: 'The improved customer environment and the better riding qualities of the new fleet will certainly benefit our existing customers and I am confident will attract new ones.'[173] That the 1938 Stock would offer 'better riding qualities' must have seemed like a reasonable expectation, given that the ride qualities of the Island's Standard Stock by this time had deteriorated to 'nothing short of abominable', according to *Rail* magazine.[174] Unfortunately it was not to be. In January 1990 *Motive Power Monthly* reported: 'Much of the Island's line is to be reballasted to improve the ride qualities of the Class 483s.'[175]

The reality was that, while test runs had shown the refurbished trains to ride well on the mainland, on the Isle of Wight, where the track at the time was largely ballasted with shingle (as was traditional for the Island), the lightweight 1938 Stock had proved if anything to ride worse than its heavier predecessors. In May 1990, when the new trains were due to take over the majority of services, a three-day shutdown of the entire line took place so that a track machine brought over from the mainland could improve the alignment of the track. This was, in the words of *Rail*, 'so that an acceptable quality of ride could be provided.'[176] One year later a special NSE supplement included with the same magazine boasted that the Island's new trains offered 'greatly enhanced quality of ride'[177] – but within three years *The Railway Magazine* would report: 'Island staff are carrying out a modification programme to bogies … to reduce rough riding.'[178] Today, almost three decades after entering service, the Island's 'bumpy trains' remain a source of amusement to tourists and young children alike.

Smallbrook Junction

As previously indicated, Lake was not the only new station to be constructed by Network SouthEast on the Isle of Wight. On 25 August 1989 NSE Director Chris Green ceremonially drove in the first key of the Isle of Wight Steam Railway's extension from Havenstreet to the site of Smallbrook Junction, promising that BR would construct an interchange station when the two lines met. Two years later, on Saturday 20 July 1991, Mr Green was back on the Island to formally declare the new 'Smallbrook Junction' station open, apparently telling the assembled crowds that the track of the newly laid extension was 'considerably better than much of his network's'![179] Supported by BR, as well as the English Tourist Board, the Rural Development Commission, Wightlink and

On the occasion of the launch into service of No 483001 on 13 July 1989, a board is unveiled at the site of the future Smallbrook Junction station by BR Isle of Wight Manager John Winkles and IWSR Chairman Stuart Page. Note that the 'proposed' station was at this stage referred to as 'Smallbrook Interchange', rather than the more heritage-friendly 'Smallbrook Junction'. *BR(S) Official, IWSR Archive*

the local councils, the extension had cost £600,000, while the joint IWSR/NSE station at Smallbrook had been built by BR over the course of eleven weeks in 1991. The first Island Line train to call at the station was the 11.32 Shanklin-Ryde service operated by veteran driver Ken West and apparently led by the hybrid unit consisting of cars Nos 123 and 224 (the same unit that had run away from Shanklin a few months earlier), with set 007 at the rear. At Smallbrook a ceremonial ribbon draped across both lines was simultaneously broken by both the Island Line train and the IWSR's flagship loco No W24 *Calbourne*, which appropriately had been Mr West's regular engine in BR steam days.

Constructed from wood in a similar fashion to Lake, Smallbrook Junction is an unusual station in being located between the tracks of the two railways and only accessible by rail; consequently Island Line trains only call at the station on days and at times when the Steam Railway is operating. Owing to the different gradients of the two lines at this location, the tracks are at different heights, only becoming level at the point of the IWSR's headshunt to the north of the station. Consequently two separate platforms are required, the Island Line platform being linked to the IWSR platform by a short upward ramp. The short Island Line platform is built for step-free access from the tube trains, while the longer IWSR's platform is constructed with conventional rolling stock in mind. Needless to say there is no physical connection between the railways; Smallbrook remains a junction in name only.

Unit No 004 calls at the then still relatively new Smallbrook Junction station in July 1993, bringing up the rear of a four-car Shanklin to Ryde Pier Head service. Access to the Steam Railway platform is on the left, past the red Network SouthEast shelter. *Martyn Hilbert*

One traditional tube feature that BR never took advantage of on the Standard Stock cars was the ability to generate extra revenue through the sale of onboard advertising space. This was quickly rectified when the 1938 Stock arrived, although this 1991 example advertising the new connection with the IWSR at Smallbrook Junction was produced in-house by Network SouthEast. Endearingly, the Island Line units are described as 'former Underground trains which have now seen the light'. *Author's collection*

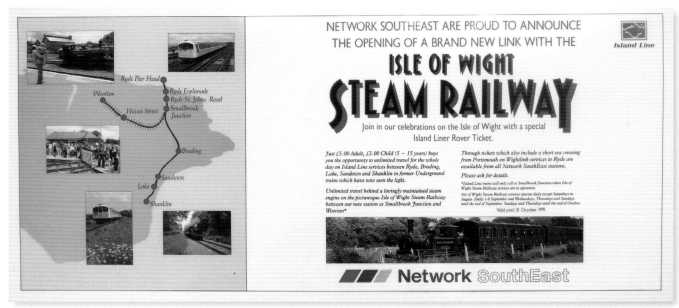

Ventnor

The opening of Smallbrook Junction arguably marked the end of Network SouthEast's transformation of the Ryde-Shanklin line. By 1991 NSE had invested more than £1.5 million[180] in its offshore operation, including replacement trains, two new stations, singling of the line between Sandown and Brading, and a £250,000 refurbishment of Ryde Works[181]. There was one investment, however, that even Network SouthEast was unwilling to consider.

Ever since 1967 the closure of the Shanklin to Ventnor line had remained for many Islanders (particularly those living in Ventnor) an injustice that had never been righted. With the NSE era ushering in a positive attitude to the Island's railways for the first time in decades, was the time finally right to reverse the cuts of the 1960s and reopen the Ventnor line? The answer was unfortunately no, with *Rail* magazine reporting in 1990 that NSE had dismissed the possibility on the grounds of cost:

> '£7 million would be required to rebuild a bridge and embankment south of Shanklin station, reinstate track and signalling, install an electric substation, provide additional rolling stock, and build a new station at the southern end.'[182]

Despite this, two years later it was reported that the Island's MP had added his support to the reopening campaign, which was now being spearheaded by the Ventnor Professional & Business Association and the Railway Development Society, and that campaigners had arranged an inspection of the tunnel under St Boniface Down.[183] In 1994 *Rail* magazine even featured a detailed 4mm scale model for a proposed new terminus at Ventnor. Commissioned by the Ventnor Railway Association, a protest group formed in the 1960s to fight the closures, the model purported to demonstrate how a new station, capable of holding a single two-car train, could be squeezed within the buildings of the industrial estate that now stood on the site of the original terminus. Although featuring a 1938 Stock unit in NSE colours, the model's creator admitted: 'Whether or not a Class 483 in Network SouthEast livery will ever make it to Ventnor, only time will tell.'[184] By 1994 the countdown to privatisation had already begun and Network SouthEast's days were numbered. If NSE was unwilling to bridge the gap to Ventnor, campaigners were wondering if another operator would take the plunge.

The fate of the Standard Stock

And what became of the Standard Stock? In 1987 only twenty-seven members of the once forty-three-strong fleet survived in service. Further withdrawals began in 1988, but the delayed arrival of the replacement 1938 Stock meant that a handful would last just into the 1990s. Vehicles were disposed of at a number of locations, some being cut up by scrap merchants at Ryde or Sandown while the majority were shipped back to Fratton for onward road transport to Vic Berry of Leicester. Throughout this period hopes were frequently raised that there might still be a place for some Standard Stock cars on the Island. Frequent mention was made in enthusiast magazines of the fact that two or more vehicles might be retained as a 'heritage set' and/or a de-icing unit. At times this prospect appeared to have the backing of NSE Director Chris Green, who revealed at the launch of No 483001 that 'one of the old Class 485 units was to be retained, possibly in a departmental fashion.'[185] This reference to Departmental use was generally taken as a reference to car No 31, which in 1971 had been fitted with Sandite equipment – the only such vehicle to be so fitted on the Island. Since none of the 1938 Stock was to have Sandite equipment, it was generally held that this vehicle at least would have to be retained – and since it was a Trailer Car (actually one of the Control Trailers that had been downgraded to a trailer for Isle of Wight use) it was assumed that driving vehicles would need to be retained to operate with it.

The end of the line for DM No 3. Withdrawn in 1989, the 1931-built vehicle awaits its date with the cutter's torch, perched precariously on top of some Mark 1 coach bodies at Vic Berry's scrapyard in Leicester, photographed some time between April 1991 and May 1992. *Andy Sansome*

In October 1990 five Standard Stock cars were transferred back to London Transport with the intention of forming a possible 'heritage set'. Pictured here at Fratton TMD on 18 October, the five-car set, including cars Nos 27 and 44, which had been externally restored at Ryde Works in vintage London Underground liveries, subsequently worked back to the capital under its own power. In the background can be glimpsed a 1938 Stock vehicle, in LT Departmental yellow livery, stored for possible Isle of Wight conversion. *David Rowland*

By the autumn of 1990 just nine cars remained on the Island. Surprisingly, for most of them at least, the immediate future looked rosy. Five vehicles had been selected by London Transport, which was looking to form its own heritage set, and these were shipped back to Fratton in early October from where they proceeded to London under their own power.

The transfer of these cars to London Underground left only four vehicles on the Island. Three of them – DM No 5, Sandite-fitted trailer No 31 and CT No 28 – were to be used as a de-icing unit 'until at least March 1991' noted *Rail* magazine. The same article had good news to report for the fourth and final vehicle, CT No 26, which 'is to be preserved by the Isle of Wight Steam Railway at Haven Street[186]. This was no random selection. Originally numbered S38S, No 26 had been the very first tube vehicle to arrive on the Isle of Wight on 1 September 1966, so held a unique position in the Island's railway history. The prospect of a move to Havenstreet would even see it reunited with 'O2' No W24 *Calbourne*, which had hauled it on a test run in 1966. Sadly it was not to be. In June 1991 *Motive Power Monthly* noted that the by now heavily graffitied vehicle was still at Ryde[187]; one month later came confirmation that 'No 26 will not now move to the Isle of Wight Steam Railway for preservation'[188]. The reality was that the IWSR at that time had neither the space nor the financial resources to take on a vehicle that had no practical use for it (it could clearly have never run it) and which required expensive asbestos removal.

Brian Hardy reports that the three-car Sandite unit comprising cars Nos 28, 31 and 5 made its last official passenger run on 12 January 1991, but continued to make de-icing runs (sometimes while carrying passengers up the pier) until 17 February 1991[189]. Official withdrawal

followed in May 1991, but the unit was maintained, although unused, during the mild winter of 1991/92, after which it was stored out of use in the down loop siding at Ryde St John's Road. None of the 1938 Stock was ever converted for Sandite duties, the work instead being taken over by a track maintenance vehicle.

In early 1994 the three cars were moved to the carriage sidings south of the station, where they joined former preservation candidate No 26. Finally, on the night of 7 April, the Island's last Standard Stock cars made their last journey when a 1938 Stock unit hauled them to Sandown, where shunter No 03079 positioned them in the non-electrified sidings of the Engineer's yard. Later that month all four cars were cut up on site by Gwent Demolition of Margam. It was a sad end of an era. Reporting on the events, *Rail* magazine said:

'Although former Shanklin line units have been preserved in London Transport guise on the mainland, many will regret that none of the Standard Stock has been retained on the Island itself.'[190]

And what of those cars 'preserved in London Transport guise'? As already stated, a five-car set, consisting of DMs Nos 2 and 7, ex-CT No 27 and trailers Nos 44 and 49, had been shipped to the mainland for onward transit to London in October 1990. Two of the vehicles, Nos 27 and 44, had already been restored to vintage Underground liveries of the 1920s and '30s before leaving Ryde Works. A formal handover took place on 3 November at Morden depot's Tube Centenary open day. Receiving the cars from Chris Green of NSE, London Underground's Managing Director Denis Tuncliffe described the vehicles as 'an important part of the underground's history'[191].

Control Trailer No 27, externally restored by the staff at Ryde Works to 1920s London Underground condition as No 1789, poses at Morden Depot Open Day on 3 November 1990. This was the event at which the five ex-Isle of Wight vehicles were formally handed over by Network SouthEast to London Underground in the hope of creating a restored LT heritage train. *Tim Brown*

In 1992 *Rail* magazine reported that London Transport had launched a 'preserved train' that would 'be displayed at LUL open days and could be made available for enthusiast rail tours.'[192] Unfortunately this was not the Standard Stock set from Ryde but rather a four-car set of restored 1938 Stock – the very same type of stock that was now running on the Isle of Wight. With an operational heritage train already in service on LU, the plan to restore the Standard Stock seemed to stall. In 1993 ownership of the former Isle of Wight cars was split up, with cars Nos 2, 7 and 44 passing to the London Underground 'Heritage' collection and Nos 49 and 27 transferred (on paper) to the custody of the London Transport Museum. The latter two cars, one a trailer and the other an ex-CT, were moved in 1998 to the LT Museum's new 'Depot' site at Acton, where they would later be joined by two DMs from the Underground's departmental fleet. With the last surviving Isle of Wight DMs no longer required by the museum, Nos 2 and 7 eventually made their way to Eastleigh in the autumn of 2011, and by February 2012 both had been broken up. A few months later trailer car No 44, one of the two vehicles actually restored to heritage livery by Ryde Works, would also meet its fate at Eastleigh.[193]

At the time of writing restoration of the LT Museum's four-car Standard Stock train, which includes what are now the only two surviving ex-Isle of Wight cars, Nos 27 and 49, remains very much a long-term project. It seems a sad fact that, almost thirty years after Ryde Works despatched an operational five-car set to London, the prospect of seeing a preserved Standard Stock train on the Underground seems as far away as ever.

Top right: Almost exactly twenty-one years after their official hand-over to London Transport for restoration, ex-Isle of Wight DMs Nos 7 and 2 stand in Eastleigh Works on 15 November 2011 awaiting asbestos removal before scrapping. Within weeks they would be reduced to bare metal. Trailer No 44 would meet the same fate a few months later. *Steve Thorpe*

Bottom right: On the same day as the previous photo a glimpse inside car No 2 reveals a perfect time capsule of Isle of Wight rail travel in the 1980s. Aside from the peeling paint and piled-up seat cushions, nothing appears to have changed in the twenty-one years since the vehicle left Ryde. *Steve Thorpe*

Privatisation

I n the autumn of 1989 it was reported that Isle of Wight bus company Southern Vectis was 'jockeying for position' with the Island's County Council to buy the Ryde-Shanklin line. Although firmly rebutted by NSE Director Chris Green, Southern Vectis was not to be put off: 'Although we have been advised that the line is not for sale, we will not give in.'[194] The railway might not have been up for sale in 1989, but as the 1980s gave way to the 1990s the situation would change rapidly.

Privatisation agenda

During the 1980s the Isle of Wight's transport network had already felt the impact of Margaret Thatcher's privatisation policies, with the Island's BR-owned Sealink ferry routes (later to become Wightlink) sold off in 1984 and Southern Vectis (previously part of the National Bus Company) passing into private hands in 1987. By the time John Major became Prime Minister in 1990 the railways had started to look like the last great privatisation for the Conservatives to

A pair of Network SouthEast-liveried units pass at Sandown on 20 March 1993. Unit No 005 is heading north towards Ryde while No 008 is forming a Shanklin service. *Andy Sansome*

tackle – and to some the recently modernised Island Line seemed an attractive proposition.

In truth there had always been something about the separate nature of the Island's railways that had attracted the interest of entrepreneurs and innovators who felt they could run things differently. The director of the London-based Austria Travel Agency had offered to take over the whole system for a nominal rent in 1963[195], while the proposed Bennie Airspeed Railway and the ill-fated Sadler-Vectrail Company have both been dealt with in earlier chapters. In September 1992, with privatisation already on the agenda, it was reported that Wightlink was in talks with the County Council with a view to taking over the Ryde-Shanklin line.[196] Just months later, in February 1993, it was announced by the Government that Island Line was to be one of the first seven rail franchises to be privatised, with a sell-off expected as early as 1994. Uniquely the Isle of Wight was to be a 'vertical franchise', with the successful new operator being responsible for the maintenance of infrastructure and signalling as well as operating the trains – 'the one isle of sanity' according to Simon Jenkins in The Times.[197]

Local consortium
Immediately the news was announced, a local consortium led by Southern Vectis and consisting of all three ferry operators, Wightlink, Red Funnel and Hovertravel, together with the Isle of Wight Steam Railway was formed with the intention of bidding for the franchise. Among the consortium's stated aims were the return of steam to Ryde Pier – with parallel running of steam and electric trains on the double-track section from Smallbrook to Ryde Pier Head – and the possible reopening of formerly closed routes. (News of the forthcoming privatisation was 'given a cautious reception' by the Ventnor Railway Association[198] – of which more later.) The consortium hoped that the line's current subsidy would continue to be guaranteed and that Ryde Pier would be made safe – NSE was currently facing a possible bill of £250,000 to replace corroded girders beneath the railway pier. Ideally the consortium also hoped to have the possibility of buying the freehold of the line rather than just be awarded a vertical franchise. Speaking to The Guardian, Southern Vectis's Managing Director, Garry Batchelor, revealed that the consortium was keen to rid the line of its 'toy railway' image and introduce new light rail vehicles to replace the existing 1938 Stock, which were 'well past their sell by date'[199]. This view of the 1938 Stock is slightly surprising considering that it had only been on the Island for about three years at the time – only the previous year Rail magazine had suggested the line's newly refurbished rolling stock 'could make it an attractive purchase'[200]. On the other hand, the trains were already around 55 years old! Speaking to Rail, Mr Batchelor implied that the steam trains would be for the tourist market while the new light rail vehicles were for the 'more serious travellers'[201].

'Disney-like'
All this talk of 'serious travellers' and losing the 'toy railway' image rung slightly hollow in May 1993 when the consortium revealed its detailed plans for the line. As quoted in Rail, the proposed light rail vehicles, together with the stations, were to be 'brightly decked-out in novelty fashion to portray a "Disney-like" image. Railway staff will be dressed as fantasy characters…'[202] The light rail vehicles were anticipated to be similar to those recently introduced on the then new Manchester Metrolink, while the proposed extension of IWSR services to the pier head was to entail a remodelling of Ryde Pier Head station and lowering of the track through Ryde Tunnel to pre-1967 levels. Also planned was a reinstatement of the passing loop at Brading. Savings were expected to be made by reducing the current staff of about sixty employees by 20%, while the consortium again made it clear that it was hoping for a complete takeover rather than just a franchise award.

Included with the article in Rail was a map of the proposed new operation, which included three new 'cheap and cheerful' stations at Whitecross (between Shanklin and Lake), Morton Common (between Sandown and Brading) and Appleby (between Ryde St John's Road and Ryde Esplanade). Ryde St John's Road itself was to be renamed Oakfield Park. Notably absent from the map was any planned reopening for the Shanklin to Ventnor section – or indeed for any other closed lines – the only new section of route instead being a proposed 'novelty' line from Brading to Sandown Esplanade. Ideas for this branch included either a monorail or an 'old tram – such as on the Isle of Man'.

At first things seemed to be going smoothly for the Southern Vectis-led consortium, which appointed a consultancy to advise on the proposed extension of the steam railway, as well as the possible replacement of the tube trains.[203] In July 1993 it was reported that BR was advertising internally for 'a highly motivated individual who either wishes to be in the vanguard of the privatisation programme or who is thinking of leaving the industry within the next two years' to serve as the Island's franchise development manager.[204] By October the consortium was still 'the only declared runner'.[205] After this, things began to slip behind.

Privatisation delayed
In January 1994 The Guardian reported that the Government's rail privatisation programme was heading for delay, with the earliest sell-off not now expected to take place until early 1995, noting also that 'an early sale of the Isle of Wight line … is also now being ruled out'. Tellingly, it also noted that the local consortium's interest had 'cooled' after being told that the Office of Fair Trading would not 'look favourably on local transport monopolies of this kind'[206]. (Since the consortium's bid would have involved all of the Island's transport operatives working together, this is not altogether surprising.) By March it was apparent that the Island had been dropped altogether from the initial batch of seven franchises to be sold, with Transport Secretary John MacGregor admitting that 'There is no firm date for the Isle of Wight yet.'[207] Two months later it became clear that the Island was to be excluded

Unit No 004 passes the outer home signal at Ryde St John's Road at the rear of a northbound four-car service on 31 July 1996, the year that Ryde-Shanklin services passed into private hands. Behind it in the headshunt No 03179, withdrawn three years earlier, is sandwiched between two ex-Waterloo & City Line adaptor wagons. *Martyn Hilbert*

from the second batch of franchises as well. There was more bad news for the consortium, with its hoped-for total buy-out being firmly ruled out by the director designate of Island Line's shadow franchise, who told staff that 'a total sale, including the infrastructure, is not on the agenda'[208]. By the summer of 1994 it was being reported that privatisation of Island Line was unlikely for 'at least' another two years – a situation that the Chairman of Southern Vectis described as 'deplorable'[209].

The end of the process

The Network SouthEast era on the Isle of Wight formally came to an end on 10 December 1995 when the shadow Island Line franchise officially took over.[210] Little difference would have been apparent to passengers, although some rebranding began to take place, with *Rail* magazine reporting in March 1996 that a new waiting shelter at Lake was to 'carry the new Island Line branding recently introduced at Ryde Esplanade'[211]. In practice, the franchise at this stage was still a wholly owned BR subsidiary, while the infrastructure, which had passed into the ownership of Railtrack in 1994, was held by the franchise on a 25-year lease. Moves towards privatisation now began to accelerate.

In mid-1996 the Southern Vectis-led consortium appeared to be holed below the waterline when it was reported that Wightlink, one of its key members, had withdrawn from the bid. By now nine other bids were on the

table including, worryingly for Southern Vectis, one from rival bus operator Stagecoach, which already held the South West Trains franchise on the mainland.[212] An invitation to tender for the franchise was issued on 27 June 1996 with the deadline for final bids to be 16 August. The initial franchise award would be only a five-year term, rather the seven-year terms on offer in other parts of the country; 'non-compliant' bids for up to fifteen years were also invited. According to *Rail's* privatisation columnist, Steve Knight, this was not a particularly attractive package:

'Just what can be done with the Island Line operation to give better value for money more than taxes my brain. You could refurbish the rolling stock, but surely what can be done with discarded London Underground trains built in 1938 must be limited and it is doubtful if the operation could afford new trains…'[213]

In August it was reported that a final 'Passenger Service Requirement' had been published for the Island Line franchise, guaranteeing the minimum service level with which any new operator must agree to comply. Protected services included early-morning trains and stops at Smallbrook Junction station to connect with IWSR services. Passenger revenue for 1995/96 was reported to be £729,000 and staff levels now stood at forty-four employees.[214] Evidently the 20% reduction in staffing levels promised by the consortium in 1993 had by now taken place under BR.

On 13 October 1996 the five-year Island Line 'vertical' franchise was finally awarded, not to the once-favoured local consortium, but instead to Stagecoach Holdings Limited.[215] Stagecoach of course already held the South West Trains franchise, meaning that, although the Isle of Wight may on paper have had its first (non-heritage) independent railway company since the 1923 Grouping, in practice the Ryde-Shanklin line was still under the same ownership as the railways on the other side of the Solent. Plus ça change.

Ventnor

Parallel to the privatisation story of the 1990s runs the rise and fall of the campaign to reopen the 4-mile Shanklin-Ventnor route. As mentioned in the previous chapter, this had been costed at £7 million when ruled out by Network SouthEast in 1990, and had subsequently become the subject of a high-profile campaign by the Ventnor Railway Association (VRA), a protest group formed in the 1960s. In the early 1990s, with the privatisation process already under way, there was much vague talk in the air, from both the County Council and the Southern Vectis-led consortium, of the possibility of reopening routes closed in the 1950s and '60s. Since this could only realistically apply to those routes that had once connected with the remaining Ryde-Shanklin line, this effectively left four options, one of which was already occupied by the Steam Railway. In practice, however, the most practical option (some might say the *only* practical option) was surely to reopen the route that almost everyone agreed should never have been closed in the first place – that from Shanklin to Ventnor. Despite this, the local consortium's plans never formally included the line to Ventnor, while the VRA itself chose to pursue its aims independently, remaining at arm's length from both the bidders and the privatisation process itself.

By August 1994 it was reported that the VRA's campaign was moving 'steadily up the political agenda'; a 'Case for Reinstatement' document had been launched 'to general acclaim' and funding was now being sought to begin a feasibility study.[216] Two months later funding had been secured – £5,000 from the County Council and £5,000 from the Rural Development Commission. With much of the route, including the tunnel under St Boniface Down, still surviving, one of the key obstacles that the study would have to examine was that of Wroxall, where the trackbed and station site had been built over by more recent development. As *Rail* magazine noted, 'One option would be a small deviation of the railway to the east of Wroxall.'[217] In December 1994 the VRA received the backing of the Civic Trust Regeneration Unit, whose own 'Action Plan for Ventnor' report claimed that the reopening campaign 'enjoyed the widest and strongest support in the town'[218]. Also recommended by the report was that the reopened station should be linked to the town's esplanade by either light rail (possibly an extension of the

line from Ryde, were that converted to light rail) or a funicular railway. (Anyone who has ever walked from Ventnor's esplanade to the site of its former station, 294 feet above sea level, will appreciate the need for such a link.) Everything now seemed to rest on the outcome of the feasibility study.

Feasibility study

On 24 January 1996, just months short of the 30th anniversary of the Ventnor line's closure, the feasibility study issued its report. Perhaps unsurprisingly, given that it was commissioned by the VRA, the study came out overwhelmingly in favour of reopening the Ventnor line. The total cost would be £9.6 million, including £3 million to construct a cut-and-cover tunnel beneath part of Wroxall. According to *Rail* magazine, the costs were based on the assumption that a half-hourly service would be operated, using the existing 1938 Stock fleet (which begs the question how the existing fleet size would have coped with the increased mileage), over a single-track formation with a passing loop at Shanklin. A diversionary route around Wroxall had been ruled out as 'it would push up the cost of reinstatement to £17.5 million'[219]. As reported by the *County Press*, the consultants and the VRA were predicting positive outcomes all round. The extended Island Line would require a smaller subsidy than was currently needed to operate the Ryde-Shanklin line, while Ventnor would once again become 'the jewel in the crown of IW seaside resorts' benefitting from an extra £836,000 tourist income per year. Wroxall would have 'considerable opportunities to attractively regenerate the core of the village.' Even the people of Shanklin would see a benefit, where reconstruction of the unlamented Landguard Manor Road Bridge would apparently 'significantly enhance this area of the town'[220].

Wroxall row

Needless to say there were a couple of downsides: first, the small matter of where the money would actually come from ('local, national and European sources with the possibility of bids for lottery and millennium funding,' said the VRA), and second, opposition from Wroxall, where people were not entirely keen to see their village turned into a construction site. Factories that had been built at the station site in Wroxall would need to be relocated – which it was feared could lead to job losses – while 'a large number of homes would be blighted' according to the Wroxall representative on the County Council. Sixteen bungalows, which had had their gardens extended over the old trackbed, would quite literally see the railway built in their backyards: 'We have spent a lot of money in our garden,' complained one resident.[221]

Relationships between Wroxall and the VRA went from bad to worse in April when it became known that a resident of Upper Ventnor (not Wroxall) had been co-opted onto the VRA to represent the views of the residents of Wroxall. The VRA probably didn't help its position when it responded, 'He may not live in Wroxall now but

By the summer of 1999 the privatised 'Island Line' franchise had been owned and operated by Stagecoach for three years, but still Network SouthEast colours reigned supreme. Unit No 009 stands at Ryde St John's Road at the rear of the 15.13 Shanklin to Ryde Pier Head service, headed by No 006 on 23 July 1999. In addition to the train's livery, NSE signage can also be seen on the platforms. *Martyn Hilbert*

he knows people there.'[222] The representative himself, initially unavailable for comment, later wrote to the *County Press* to point out that he was born and raised in Wroxall and that most of his extended family still lived there, proffering the unlikely opinion that 'the reinstated railway will serve Wroxall probably better than Ventnor, initially at any rate.'[223] Things had little improved by July, when it was reported that the VRA had invited Wroxall Parish Council to join a working group, but had not invited them to a progress meeting at County Hall. According to one parish councillor, the VRA was 'full of nice words' but 'its performance in both the past and present was somewhat lacking.' The VRA, for its part, claimed that 'relevant organisations' would be fully consulted after the £7 million Millennium Fund bid had been considered. In the end it was this bid, and not the problem of Wroxall, that would sink the VRA's proposal.

Bid refused

In February 1997 the Ventnor extension hit the buffers when it was announced that the Millennium Commission had turned down the VRA's bid for £7 million towards the cost. (Interestingly the *County Press* was now referring to 'the £14 million plans' rather than the almost £10 million

suggested by the feasibility study only one year previously.) The VRA was putting on a brave face – 'this is a setback, but no more than that' – and announced that it would be considering applications for European and Lottery funding. The County Council member for Wroxall was quick to put the knife in:

'It is all right for people to dream in Technicolor and live in fairyland when they use their own money but when they are using taxpayers' money to keep these dreams going it is annoying. These people have already blighted the selling prospects of 15 to 20 bungalows at Wroxall.'[224]

One week later the VRA announced that it was preparing a 'heritage-based' bid for lottery funding, but in truth little more seems to have been heard of the extension plans after that. Two years later the Island Line's controller told *The Times*:

'A new Ventnor extension is often talked about, but whether that will come, I just don't know. Studies will have to be undertaken to look for a cost-effective way forward.'[225]

From left to right, withdrawn cars Nos 121, 223, 125 and 222 can be seen grounded in the car park at Ryde St John's Road on 23 July 1999. Note that some of the cars have been rotated, creating the unusual sight of a 'D' end cab facing the same way as an 'A' end cab. All four would be scrapped the following year. *Martyn Hilbert*

Rolling stock and service levels

By the time the Island Line franchise passed into private hands in October 1996, Network SouthEast's original service of three trains per hour had long since passed into history. In May 1993, only one year since the delivery of unit No 483009 and two spare cars, the Ryde-Shanklin service was reduced to just two trains per hour. For the first time the lack of a passing loop at Brading became an issue with the introduction of the since-familiar irregular service pattern of 20/40-minute intervals. A three-train service was restored for the peak summer season, but that autumn the winter service was reduced to only one train an hour, with BR now being forced to deny rumours that the Sunday service was in danger of being axed altogether.[226] Meanwhile the once-familiar Ryde Pier shuttle had ceased regular operation in 1991, only to be briefly revived (depending on crew availability) for the summer of 1997. Clearly, with service levels reduced there was no longer the requirement for as many two-car units.

On 28 January 1994 unit No 483005 collided with the buffer stops at Ryde Pier Head, causing damage to DM No 125. Unit No 483003 was also out of service at the time owing to defects with car No 223, so the serviceable cars from both units were paired to create one 'good' unit, which took the number 483003. Unit No 483005, now consisting of the two unserviceable cars, was stored out of service and soon became the first unit to be withdrawn. Further withdrawals followed swiftly, with unit No 483003 (consisting of cars Nos 123 and 221) being withdrawn in May 1995, and No 483001 (consisting of cars Nos 121 and 222) following in June 1996.

By the time Stagecoach took control of Island Line only six operational units (twelve vehicles) remained in service. As was normal on the privatised railway, the operational units were actually owned by a private Rolling Stock Operating Company, in this case Eversholt Leasing, which in turn leased the stock back to the operator, Stagecoach. Also at Ryde were withdrawn units Nos 483001, 003 and 005, from which four cars, Nos 121, 125, 222 and 223, were lifted from their bogies and dumped in the car park on 1 March 1998, where they were joined shortly after by the two cars of 'spare' unit No 483010. (At this point, with the formations of the withdrawn units mixed and most of their carriages lying side by side on the ground, it becomes easier to talk of individual car numbers rather than unit numbers.) Cars Nos 121, 125, 222 and 223 were scrapped in situ in May 2000. Withdrawn cars Nos 123 and 221, initially held as a strategic reserve, remained in a siding to the north of Ryde St John's Road until broken up in June 2006. Spare

Also seen grounded at Ryde St John's Road on the same day is the never-required 'spare set' No 010. Somewhat bizarrely the all-over-blue cars appear to have been festooned with bunting in the red, white and blue colours of Network SouthEast – quite possibly left over from the launch of the Island's 1938 Stock ten years earlier! *Martyn Hilbert*

unit No 483010 was also scrapped, although the author has not been unable to determine precisely when.

Branding

In the early years of privatisation little was done in the way of rebranding the franchise. During 1996, even before Stagecoach took over, the shadow franchise began applying new 'Island Line' signage and house colours – described by *Rail* as 'magnolia and blue'[227] – to its stations. The trains, however, which of course had been branded 'Island Line' since their launch in 1989, remained stubbornly in NSE colours until the end of the decade. Interestingly, since Stagecoach also owned the adjacent and much larger South West Trains franchise, no attempt was made to apply SWT branding to the Island's trains.

A fitter waits on the platform to carry out a minor repair to unit No 009 as it arrives at Ryde St John's Road en route to Shanklin on 27 June 2001. By this time the station has received Island Line's magnolia and blue house colours, although NSE signage remains in place. *Andy Sansome*

Unit No 006 leads No 009 forming the 15.23 Shanklin to Ryde Pier Head service, seen here departing from Ryde St John's Road on 14 July 2002. In the former down loop can be seen withdrawn cars Nos 123 and 221, still in NSE livery and partly sheeted over so as not to present an eyesore to the occupants of neighbouring houses. Initially retained as a strategic reserve, these withdrawn vehicles were later scrapped in 2006. *Martyn Hilbert*

Most reliable railway

The privatisation era on the Isle of Wight did not get off to a good start. In December 1997, little more than a year after Stagecoach had taken over, *The Times* reported that the new operators had been fined £7,200 after Island Line had seen 'the most rapid deterioration in punctuality with one in every 20 of its services running late.'[228] This situation was reversed just months later when the paper revealed that, while ScotRail was to be named as the most punctual franchise in *mainland* Britain, it had nonetheless been 'pipped by the Isle of Wight's eight-mile line'[229]. Remarkably this position as the most reliable franchise in terms of both punctuality and number of cancellations was one that Island Line would retain for much of its time as a separate franchise.

Needless to say, the comparison between a single isolated 8-mile end-to-end railway line and any of the large interconnected networks that made up the privatised national network of mainland Britain was hardly a fair one, but it did guarantee the franchise a degree of national media attention whenever the figures were released. As *The Times* put it in 1999:

'League tables, like statistics, take no account of weighting by capacity or clientele, and while Virgin Cross Country receives 890 complaints per 100,000 journeys (123,251 moans), Island Line gets only ten complaints per 100,000 journeys (a total of 72). So there it is: Island Line stands at the top of the league.'

The same article, while full of praise for the staff, goes on to describe how the 'ancient, worm-eaten trains' were 'being run into the ground' according to one of the drivers. The paintwork was 'rusty' and the windows 'smeary and lacklustre'. By now only thirty-five staff were employed, and even the line's manager, Alan Cracknell, admitted, 'It really is a rolling museum… It will reach the end of its useful life in 2003.'[230]

Dinosaur trains

In the year 2000 a £1 million refurbishment of the remaining six units included the introduction of a startling new livery, featuring colourful dinosaurs roaming a prehistoric landscape. Launched to the media on 21 March 2000, thirty-three years to the day since the launch of the Island's first tube trains into passenger service, the new livery, which included a prominent 'Stagecoach Island Line' logo, was achieved through the application of vinyl images over a painted base colour of blue. Notably this was the first time since the 1920s that the Isle of Wight's trains were painted in something other than the house colours of the mainland railways, and the Island's first ever livery to be designed specifically with the tourist trade in mind.

Four months after the launch of the controversial 'dinosaur' livery, freshly repainted unit No 004 heads south from Ryde Esplanade on 18 July 2000 with the 07.42 Ryde Pier Head to Shanklin service. Even this early on the unit is clearly not carrying a dinosaur-themed name in its destination box. A further splash of colour is provided by the blue-painted Southern Vectis 'Island Explorer' Leyland Olympian bus in the adjacent bus station. *Martyn Hilbert*

Departing north from Smallbrook Junction on 27 June 2001, unit No 009 is followed by No 002, which proudly displays its 'Raptor' name – quite possibly the only unit to regularly carry its allocated dinosaur name. The dinosaur livery was certainly not the best livery to be carried by the Island's 1938 Stock but, as some of these pictures show, when new it could still look quite attractive. *Andy Sansome*

A four-car dinosaur-liveried formation, consisting of units Nos 009 and 002, waits at Smallbrook Junction with a southbound service on 27 June 2001. The station itself appears to be still very much in NSE condition. *Andy Sansome*

By 2007, when this photo was taken at Ryde St John's Road on 5 August, the five dinosaur-liveried units were looking decidedly unkempt and rusty. Repairs to the paintwork on unit No 006 have caused the dinosaur on the cabside to be decapitated! *Author*

This interior shot of car No 129 from unit 009 was taken at Shanklin on 27 June 2001. By this time No 009 had been externally repainted in dinosaur livery but still retains its original NSE interior. Other than a change of moquette, this view would be largely unaltered today. *Andy Sansome*

The 'Stagecoach Island Line' logo as applied to the five dinosaur units is seen here on the side of unit No 006 at Ryde St John's Road on 5 August 2007 – where it is in danger of being overwhelmed by a large patch of rust. *Author*

Intended to capitalise on the then recent transmission of the BBC series *Walking with Dinosaurs*, as well as the Island's own dinosaur heritage[231], the livery inevitably drew comparison with the almost prehistoric age of the trains themselves. As the *County Press* put it, 'the 62-year-old trains on the Island are dinosaurs – and now they look like them,' before going on to note that, while five of the six remaining units had been repainted, 'the sixth is being painted in London Underground colours to reflect its past operating on the Northern Line.'[232]

The five units to carry the dinosaur livery were Nos 002, 004, 006, 008 and 009, and these were allocated the names 'Raptor', 'Terry' (short for Pterodactyl), 'T-Rex', 'Iggy' and 'Bronti'. The names were displayed in the destination box, in addition to the destination, although the photographic evidence (and the author's memory) suggests that – with the exception of No 002 'Raptor' – most names were not carried for very long, if at all. To accompany the new livery, signage was now installed at stations incorporating the dinosaur motif.

An example of the dinosaur-themed signage applied to Island Line stations in the era of the dinosaur–liveried trains, photographed at Shanklin on 28 May 2006. *Author*

Perhaps unsurprisingly, the cartoonish livery did not go down very well with some *County Press* readers, who suggested instead that the £1 million spent on refurbishment might have been better invested in new trains or even investigating the possibility of reopening closed lines. One reader, who remarked that 'the new livery on the IslandLine (sic) train is horrible,' felt the news that one unit was to receive Underground livery didn't go far enough:

'…at least paint them all into the London Underground colours to reflect trains past on the Northern Line, creating a Heritage Line? Bring back the old London Underground livery please and leave the dinosaurs extinct…'[233]

This person at any rate would eventually get their wish granted.

Red trains

The unit initially selected to receive London Underground red livery was No 007, which, having never carried dinosaur livery, became both the last Island unit to carry NSE colours and the first to be repainted red. Having been taken out of service in May 2000, the unit was repainted during August and was almost ready to re-enter traffic when, in October 2000, it was badly damaged when Ryde Works was hit by severe flooding. (Ryde Works, like Ryde Tunnel, has a history of flooding due to the proximity of Monktonmead Brook – the same 'small brook' that gives Smallbrook Junction its name.) Major work had to be undertaken to get the unit operational again, while both cars required a further repaint after being vandalised in June 2001. Finally in January 2003, more than two years later than originally planned, the restored unit re-entered traffic.

As released in 2003, No 007 was in as authentic as possible a recreation of the 1938 Stock's original London Transport red livery, aside from the obligatory yellow end required by Network Rail. The pillars between the windows were painted cream, while the carriages carried 'London Transport' branding and their original LT numbers – car No 127 reverted to No 10291 and car No 227 became 11291. (These numbers and the external LT branding have both been lost in later repaints.) The windows received authentic LT roundel 'No Smoking' signs, while internally the seats were reupholstered with an LT moquette. Strictly speaking the moquette used was historically incorrect for the 1938 Stock as it was actually that fitted to refurbished Metropolitan Line trains during the 1990s (as with the use of D Stock moquette in the 1980s, its appearance on the Island probably reflected Ryde's reliance on Acton Works as its main source of spares), but it certainly helped to give the unit an authentic 'Underground' feel. The five dinosaur units continued to use NSE moquette.

On 007's release into traffic, Island Line's General Manager told *Island Rail News*:

'We have gone to great lengths to achieve an authentic look for 007. No 007 will be the only operational example of its class anywhere carrying the 1938 livery. It is unique and should attract a lot of interest.'[234]

No 007 would not retain its unique status for long. Later in 2003 a second unit, No 009, was also repainted into LT livery, the two units sometimes being operated in multiple to provide a four-car red train. On this occasion the carriages retained their TOPS numbers and did not receive LT branding or roundels – meaning that it could be argued that only 007 was in *true* LT livery. (Transport for London is, of course, very protective of its logos and copyrights, so it may well be that it had only given permission for one Island unit to carry its branding.) The other four units would continue to carry dinosaur livery for several years to come.

Four months after being re-released into traffic, an immaculate London Transport-liveried No 007 stands at Shanklin on 25 May 2003. The prominent letter 'D' indicates that this is the unit's D-end cab. Originally carried on the NSE-liveried 1938 Stock, the letters 'A' or 'D' were painted over during the dinosaur era but reinstated with the onset of red livery. *Nick Doolan collection*

The Final Years of Tube Train Operation?

On 4 February 2007 Island Line ceased to exist as an individual rail franchise, instead being merged into an extended South Western franchise. For the Isle of Wight this was very much a case of 'meet the new boss/same as the old boss', as the new franchise remained in the hands of Stagecoach, which continued to market its mainland services as 'South West Trains' and its Island service as 'Island Line'. (It did, however, mean that, as it was no longer a separate franchise, the Ryde-Shanklin line ceased to appear in national league tables of rail performance.) With new trains still not on the horizon, the line increasingly began to resemble a working museum, with stations and trains soon decked out in 'heritage' colours.

Trains for £1.00

One of Stagecoach's first moves following the launch of the extended franchise was to purchase a fleet of trains for its Ryde-Shanklin operation. This was not a new fleet, however, but merely the twelve vehicles that were already operating the line; the 1938 Stock cars were acquired from their previous owner HSBC Rail (as Eversholt Leasing was known at the time) for the token sum of only £1.00.

For Stagecoach this made very good financial sense since the company had previously leased the trains for £140,000 per year, meaning that they had paid HSBC more than £1 million in the years since privatisation. One can only assume that HSBC for its part was glad to be rid of the responsibility for such elderly rolling stock. A formal handover took place in front of the press at Ryde Works on 23 March 2007 with representatives from Stagecoach and HSBC exchanging a contract in return for a £1 coin.

Having effectively acquired a free fleet of trains, Stagecoach clearly intended to make the most of them, with Island Line's General Manager Andy Naylor telling the *County Press*: 'We will undoubtedly be running the trains until the end of our recently renewed ten-year franchise.' Stating that 'the dinosaur livery has probably had its day,' he revealed that Stagecoach intended to 'make the best' of its elderly fleet by 'making a feature of their rail heritage.'[236]

Heritage liveries

This intended promotion of the trains as a heritage feature meant a repaint for the entire fleet into the London Transport red livery already carried by units Nos 007 and

Contrasting front ends at Ryde St John's Road on 8 February 2008: on the left unit No 004 (masquerading as '400') is newly outshopped in full Island Line-style red livery with yellow ends, while on the right out-of-service unit No 002 has been repainted without yellow ends, giving it an altogether more authentic version of LT livery. No 002, which still retains its 'Raptor' dinosaur name, did eventually receive yellow ends but is believed never to have worked in service again. *Andrew Long*

By the summer of 2008 the only unit remaining in dinosaur livery was No 006, seen here at Sandown looking rather sorry for itself en route to Shanklin on 30 July that year. *Andrew Long*

By 6 March 2009 No 006 had become the final unit to succumb to LT-style red livery, and is seen looking very smart at Lake. The station too has clearly been refurbished with new signage and a newly resurfaced platform. Note that once repainted, No 006 initially ran without white handrails and with red instead of cream between the passenger windows. *Andrew Long*

A recently repainted No 009 waits at Shanklin on 2 July 2009. Note that the unit has received white-painted handrails on the side of the cab but not the front. Many comments have been made about the sometimes poor external condition of the Island's 1938 Stock units in recent years, but with a fresh coat of paint they still look as good as this. *Andrew Long*

009. Repaints, which were sponsored by HSBC as part of the handover deal, quickly got under way, with the final dinosaur unit, No 006, being outshopped in red during the winter of 2008-09. Included in the repaints was unit No 002, which was stored at Ryde, apparently out of use since 2004, and which initially received LT-style red without yellow warning panels on the cabs, presenting an altogether more authentic version of the Underground livery. Despite this, the application of LT livery to No 002 was never fully completed; the uprights between the windows remain to this day in the blue colour of the dinosaur livery. By 2009 yellow ends had been applied, although the unit is believed never to have worked in passenger service again.

It was not just the trains that were to be restored to heritage colours. Reporting that the trains were to be repainted, the 23 March 2007 edition of the *County Press* had also noted there were 'plans to repaint some of the stations on the line'[237]. Six months later the paper announced that a £200,000 investment in the stations had been promised and that they would be 'repainted in the heritage colours of green and cream and new seats installed.'[238] One station, however, was already in heritage colours.

The restoration of Brading

As reported in Chapter Six, the previously derelict station building on the up platform at Brading had been restored and transformed into a community centre in 1989. Unfortunately by the turn of the century history seemed to be repeating itself, with the building once more becoming run-down and vandalised. In 2003 a meeting of Brading Town Council and other interested parties (including the Isle of Wight Steam Railway) was told that

A view inside the cab of car No 226, the 'A' end of unit No 006, seen at Shanklin on 29 March 2016. Network SouthEast moquette is still in place on the driver's seat. *Nick Doolan*

In the tranquil surroundings of Brading station in July 2014, the direction sign, standing on the trackbed of the former down line, shows the current white-on-green Island Line signage, while behind it the redundant island platform, cleared of vegetation by volunteers from the IWSR, has been restored to the green-and-cream colours of the steam era. The bench on Platform 2, which is inaccessible to the public, is often occupied by a mannequin reading a newspaper! *Martyn Hilbert*

Visitors taking a guided tour of the restored signal box at Brading are also shown around the disused island platform, affording the opportunity to photograph trains from Platform 2 for the first time since the 1980s. Here unit No 008 arrives with a Shanklin-bound service on 5 September 2013. The third-rail from the former down line, retained to assist with running rail return resistance, can clearly be seen. *Author*

Unit No 004 departs north from Brading station as the 17.38 Shanklin to Ryde Pier Head service on 3 July 2018. The previously redundant footbridge currently provides access for guided tours of the restored signal box, but if the long-proposed passing loop is ever installed here it may one day serve passengers using Platform 2 again. *Martyn Hilbert*

the cost of 'repair and converting the station into a heritage centre and meeting room' was an estimated £70,000.[239] Treated as a priority by the Council, grant aid was now sought and won, and in 2005 the restored up platform building was reopened to the public. Repainted in steam-era green and cream livery (which ironically it had still carried as recently as the late 1980s), the revitalised building now offered light refreshments, tourist information, internet access, bicycle hire and a railway heritage exhibition, and was described by the *County Press* as 'probably … the best tiny rural railway station in the country'[240]. One year later the station was honoured in the IW Society Conservation Awards.[241] In 2007 the IWSR assisted by clearing almost two decades worth of vegetation from the former island platform and surrounding area, while further grants have allowed the restoration of the down platform building and disused signal box – both of which have been open to the public for guided tours since 2010. In summer months a mannequin can often be seen seated on the disused Platform 2, reading a newspaper and waiting for a train that never comes.

Heritage stations

With Brading already in heritage colours, it is perhaps not surprising that a similar scheme was chosen in 2007 for the other seven stations on the line. Unlike Brading, however, the scheme chosen this time was a rather more generic green and cream livery, with red trimmings, seeking to ape rather than faithfully replicate the colour schemes of the steam era. New green-on-white signage was also introduced, including BR-style totems, albeit with lettering in the 'Brunel' typeface used across the South West Trains network rather than the Gill Sans of actual BR totems. In fact, the use of totems at all is surprising given that very few Isle of Wight stations ever received BR totems, and probably none of those on the Ryde-Shanklin line – several of which were still carrying Southern Railway 'targets' at the start of the 1970s. Today there are far more Isle of Wight stations carrying BR-style totems than was ever the case in the BR era. (Smallbrook Junction, built in 1991, now has the distinction of carrying both SR-style targets, on the IWSR platform, and BR-style totems on the Island Line platform.) Totems aside, signage now consists of green signs with a white border and white lower-case Brunel lettering.

One surprising aspect of the new green signage is the amount of somewhat unnecessary platform number signs installed – given that most stations now only have one operational platform. Shanklin, for example, has a prominently numbered

This example of the 'retro' British Railways-style totems now used at all stations on the Ryde-Shanklin line is seen at Brading on 27 August 2008. Ironically very few Isle of Wight stations actually carried this style of signage in the BR era. *Author*

Left: This timetable leaflet from 2011 shows the SWT-style 'Island Line Trains' logo used on publicity material during the later years of Stagecoach operation, but never displayed on the exterior of trains. *Author's collection*

Below: A good impression of the current Island Line combination of green and cream paintwork, green signage and red trains is given by this shot of Ryde St John's Road during the afternoon of 3 July 2016. Unit No 006 is stabled outside the depot adjacent to Platform 3 while the photographer is standing in the station car park next to Platform 1, where the steam loco shed once stood. *Martyn Hilbert*

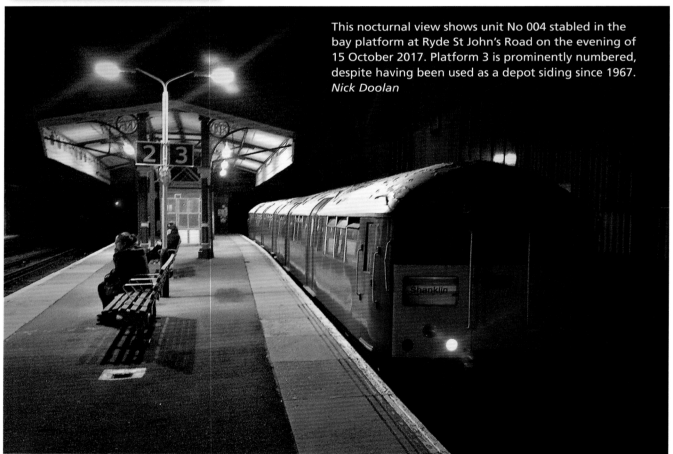

This nocturnal view shows unit No 004 stabled in the bay platform at Ryde St John's Road on the evening of 15 October 2017. Platform 3 is prominently numbered, despite having been used as a depot siding since 1967. *Nick Doolan*

Above: Shanklin station appears unexpectedly verdant on 16 May 2015, as No 004 prepares to depart for Ryde. Trees have sprung up where once the tracks continued over the former Landguard Manor Road Bridge, while the landscaped remains of Platform 2 can be glimpsed on the right. Note that the one remaining platform has been prominently numbered '1' in the latest style of signage, despite the fact that Platform 2 has been out of use and partially demolished for decades. *R. S. Freeman*

Overleaf: Unit No 007 makes its way down Ryde Pier, the LT roundels in its windows silhouetted by the sunset, forming the 20.07 Ryde Pier Head to Shanklin service on 26 June 2013. *Martyn Hilbert*

Platform 1 – despite the fact that the half-demolished remains of Platform 2 are barely visible to the casual observer. Lake has its sole platform numbered despite having never had more than one platform, while conversely Smallbrook Junction, which actually has two platforms – one for Island Line and one for the steam railway – carries no platform numbers on either line. At Ryde St John's Road the former Platform 3 has regained its number despite having seen little, if any, passenger use since becoming a stabling siding in 1967.

Repainting was undertaken quickly so that in June 2008 the *County Press* was able to report that 'stations now have their frontages decorated in heritage colours in time for the main holiday season.'[242] What was not mentioned was that one station had avoided redecoration. For some years Ryde Esplanade had been allowed to become increasingly run-down in expectation of a multi-million-pound rebuild.

'Ryde Gateway'

In 2001 the SRA report noted:

'A proposal for a new transport interchange terminal at the Ryde Esplanade would replace the existing main station building. The development of this scheme is at an early stage but is being developed by IOW Council with implementation by 2004/5.'[243]

The proposal for a new interchange, or 'Gateway', had originated the previous year after a successful Council bid for £6.25 million in Government funds to regenerate the town: 'Ambitious ideas under consideration include a new bus and train interchange,' reported the *County Press*.[244] By the following year detailed plans were being drawn up 'to incorporate road, rail and sea transport services into one easy stop at the new Ryde Interchange.'[245] This would involve demolishing the Victorian railway station,

which incorporated parts of the original tramway station, as well as the attached 1970s bus station.

In 2005 a competition to design the new interchange, which would be used by 'ferry, hovercraft, train, bus, taxi and coach passengers, plus pedestrians and cyclists' was won by the architects of the London Eye with a 'futuristic interlocking leaf design' – although the Council's project manager was quick to point out that the winning design was 'probably not what the public will get'[246]. After this, the station began to take on an increasingly derelict appearance, as existing shops and facilities were vacated and boarded up in preparation for forthcoming demolition. In 2006 *The Railway Magazine* reported that the new interchange was expected to open in October/November 2007, following a six-month closure of the station.[247]

Instead delays now set in, with the *County Press* reporting in December 2007 that construction, now expected to begin in January 2008, was likely to be postponed further due to 'contractual issues' over land ownership.[248] Two months later the expected redevelopment was looking 'increasingly distant', with the existing bus station, expected to be replaced by temporary bus stops along the Esplanade, being repainted and brought back into use while news broke that the vacant shop units were to be re-let.[249] In October 2009 the *County Press* reported that the 'Gateway' project, which had already cost the Council £1.6 million, was to be axed: 'Faced with spiralling costs and lack of agreement with Esplanade rail and bus station owner Network Rail, the IW Council's cabinet is being recommended … to finally pull the plug.'[250]

With the multi-million-pound project cancelled, subsequent developments at Ryde Esplanade have been rather more low-key. In 2010 it was reported that Network Rail had been put under pressure by Transport Secretary Lord Adonis to improve the increasingly decrepit station[251], and by 2013 the station had been repainted into the same green and cream 'heritage' colour scheme, complete with totems, as the rest of the line. The disused Platform 2, once the sole preserve of the former pier shuttle service, has been truncated by the removal of the section that formerly extended over the pier. The platform still appears to be long enough to hold a two-car train, but it has seen no further use and is unlikely ever to do so unless either the pier shuttle is reinstated or the current pointwork is relocated from the south to the north of the station. In 2015 the Isle of Wight Community Rail Partnership, founded in 2005, began an ongoing project to landscape the abandoned Platform 2 with raised planting beds.

Island-based company?

With the stations and trains in heritage colours and Brading station offering tours of its restored signal box, it seemed that the Ryde-Shanklin line was destined to resemble ever more a tourist attraction, albeit only the second-best heritage railway on the Isle of Wight. However, change was in the air when, in August 2014, the *County Press* reported: 'An Island-based company running Island Line is one possibility to save the railway for future generations.'[252] This would prove to be the opening act of a political debacle that by the following summer would see Islanders fearing for the continued existence of the Ryde-Shanklin line, while the *County Press* ran front-page headlines reading 'Save Our Trains'[253]. How did things go so wrong so quickly?

Task force

The 'Island-based company' suggestion was one of the ideas floated at a meeting of Island Line 'stakeholders', including South West Trains and the Isle of Wight Council, held in August 2014 to discuss the long-term future of the Ryde-Shanklin line beyond the expiry of SWT's franchise in 2017. Contacted by the *County Press*, a Department for Transport spokesman confirmed that 'no decision had been made on the size and shape of the future South West Trains franchise but people were being consulted about their aspirations for Island Line.'[254] Later that year it was reported that the local MP, Andrew Turner, was planning to create a transport 'task force' to consider all of the Island's transport needs and that the idea had already won the backing of the transport minister. The scheme was 'unanimously applauded' at a meeting of the Council although a suggestion by one councillor that this could lead to the return of steam trains on the main line was dismissed as 'pure and utter fantasy'[255]. Three weeks later, in December 2014, the *County Press* ran the front-page headline 'Steaming Back into Ryde?'

'Top-level discussions' were now said to have been taking place between Andrew Turner MP and the Government for the past year; 'which could result in the transfer of the Island Line franchise from South West Trains to the Island community and run by a social enterprise partnership.' Mr Turner was to meet with rail minister Claire Perry in February to discuss the creation of a task force with DfT funding 'with a remit to secure the future of the railway'. Proposals under consideration were said to include de-electrification of the Ryde-Shanklin line and the introduction of replacement diesel trains, 'allowing steam trains to once again run into Ryde Esplanade station'. Operation to Ryde Pier Head was ruled out as steam trains would be 'too heavy' for the pier in its current condition. According to the *County Press*, the Isle of Wight Steam Railway's General Manager 'supported the idea in principle', but was keen to stress that Ryde St John's Road was 'a more realistic aim' and that steam trains could not operate to Esplanade 'as long as electric trains ran in Ryde Tunnel'.[256] By this stage the DfT was planning to extend SWT's franchise until 2019 – also the year in which the 25-year lease on Island Line's infrastructure was due to expire.

Steam ambitions

What were the Steam Railway's ambitions and how would future changes to Island Line make it possible for steam to return to Ryde St John's Road? In fact, this had long been, and continues to be, an aim of the railway. Writing to the *County Press* in January 2015, the IWSR's Commercial Manager Jim Loe stated that 'the suggestion the steam railway be extended into Ryde first came from South West

Trains … in 2009.'[257] However, a 2004 article by the IWSR's then Chairman John Suggett reveals that the idea had been suggested by Network SouthEast at the time of the construction of the Smallbrook extension and raised again by the IWSR when asked to contribute to a Rail Passengers Committee document in 2002:

'Our view was that Island Line should be converted to light rail and be operated by diesel trams, with the Steam Railway having exclusive use of one line between Smallbrook and Ryde St John's.'[258]

In reality this scenario could only be made possible if Island Line's passing loop at Sandown was moved to a position at or near Brading, to allow a 30-minute-interval service between Ryde and Shanklin (the halfway point on the line being just north of Brading). As Jim Loe's 2015 letter explains, 'With trains only passing at Brading, Island Line would no longer need the double track between Smallbrook Junction and Ryde St John's Road, and the redundant "up" track would have become available.' With Ryde St John's Road becoming an interchange between the two railways, Smallbrook Junction would have become redundant and been closed. Mr Loe was keen to stress that 'The two railways would have remained totally separate, running parallel for the mile into St John's Road.'[259] (Interestingly, this would have mirrored the original, pre-Grouping arrangement, when the Isle of Wight Railway and Isle of Wight Central Railway also ran on two separate parallel tracks between Smallbrook and Ryde St John's Road.) The letter does not discuss the possible layout of Ryde St John's Road in the event of such an arrangement, but it is worth noting that the station currently retains three platform faces (one of them presently occupied by a siding). If IWSR trains were to enter the existing station without crossing any Island Line tracks they would have to access the current up platform – and even then a run-round loop (possibly occupying the current down platform) would be required if top-and-tailing of steam trains was to be avoided.

Ministerial approval

The previously announced meeting between Island MP Andrew Turner and rail minister Claire Perry took place in February 2015, with the minister giving 'a green light to further develop the business plan for the community-operated rail service.' Officials from the DfT advised the *County Press* that 'the intention was to extend South West Trains' current franchise for the railway until 2019, but plans for the service beyond that date were uncertain.'[260]

It is worth stating at this point that there appears to be no evidence that the DfT had ever considered removing the Ryde-Shanklin line from the South Western franchise until it was suggested to it by the Island's MP. It certainly was not proposing this with any lines on the mainland. Nonetheless the Conservative-led coalition Government was keen to make savings, and when the idea was presented to it as a positive and desirable move by one of its own MPs, accompanied by several senior members of the Island's Conservative-run Council, it is not surprising that the minister was happy to approve.

Surprisingly, the future of Island Line does not appear to have been much of an issue for any of the local candidates in that year's General Election, which saw Andrew Turner returned to office on 7 May 2015. However, within two months a growing body of opinion began to form that what Mr Turner was encouraging the DfT to do might not be such a good idea after all…

Fears

On 3 July 2015 the *County Press* reported that Council leader Jonathan Bacon had been quizzed by Island Line employee Lee Wilson, expressing fears that handing the railway over to a community-owned company would have a negative impact on jobs and services. In response Mr Bacon (who had been part of the delegation that accompanied Andrew Turner in his February meeting with the rail minister) stated:

'My preferred option would be keeping the railway under the current arrangements but we have to look at something else. What we are looking at is trying to maintain rail services and retain jobs and a rail industry. The alternative would be to have no rail service.'[261]

Just one week later came the news that the DfT had been unable to reach an agreement with Stagecoach over extending the South Western franchise until 2019; if Island Line was to be removed from the franchise it now seemed likely to happen in 2017. As the Mayor of Shanklin noted: 'It's a bombshell. We now have to find a solution to the problem in the next two years.' Cllr Bacon meanwhile, in apparent contradiction to what he had said the previous week, advised the *County Press* that 'he still believed the most effective rail service for the Island would be through a community ownership model.'[262] Elsewhere in the same issue was a letter from David Pugh, himself a former Conservative leader of the Council, expressing concerns that the policies of Cllr Bacon and Andrew Turner MP would leave Island Line 'decimated following removal from a supporting rail franchise'. According to Mr Pugh, being part of the SWT franchise allowed Island Line to be underwritten by more profitable lines elsewhere:

'Mr Turner talks of our service losing around £3 million a year (a figure he has not substantiated), but this is a red herring. Island Line is part of a healthy, fully viable franchise – and is fortunate to be underwritten by this wider network, just like many other rural routes across the south…

Here on the Island, our representatives seem to be giving ministers the green light to wash their hands of our local service.

Nothing good can come of this. If Island Line does makes an operational loss along the lines of what the

MP claims, it would be impossible for it to survive on its own and maintain the same levels of service.

The only viable option is for Island Line to remain part of the South Western franchise.'[263]

Mr Pugh's letter would prove to be the start of an ongoing campaign.

'Save Our Trains'

On 17 July 2015 the *County Press* dedicated its front page to a story headlined 'Save Our Trains'. The article itself had little new to say; however, political manoeuvres continued on the Letters page. Island Line employee Lee Wilson wrote to say that he had still had no straightforward replies to his concerns from either the MP or Cllr Bacon, while the councillor defended himself against the claims made by David Pugh the previous week. Asserting that his 'preferred option' was to keep the line within the existing franchise, he now distanced himself from the MP's policies, stating: 'I have set out my position and Mr Turner and ministers can set out theirs.' Elsewhere on the same page, former Labour Party candidate Stewart Blackmore had written in to say that he agreed 'with most of what David Pugh writes'[264]. The following week would see Pugh and Blackmore join forces to form a cross-party campaign to the keep the Ryde-Shanklin line within the South Western franchise.

Subsidy

Much talk was made in the front-page article of 17 July of Island Line being in receipt of an annual '£3 million subsidy' although, as Mr Pugh had implied the previous week, this was a somewhat moot point. Since the line was no longer a franchise in its own right it no longer received any direct subsidy from the Government. Instead the line was funded by the South Western franchise holder, Stagecoach, which, like other rail franchises, received a much larger Government subsidy to maintain legally specified minimum service levels on all those lines that were deemed loss-making but socially necessary. David Pugh claimed that the £3 million figure was unsubstantiated, but how much was it costing Stagecoach to run the Ryde-Shanklin line? Back in 2000, when Island Line had been a separate franchise (and was still leasing its rolling stock at £140,000 per year) it was reported to be receiving a £2 million Government subsidy.[265] Allowing for 15 years' worth of declining infrastructure and the ever-increasing costs of maintaining rolling stock that was now nearly 80 years old, not to mention rising inflation, the oft-quoted figure of £3 million (in return for only £1 million annual return) seems not unreasonable. If removal from the franchise (and by implication, it was feared, the national rail network) was to mean the end of Government subsidy, where instead was this money to come from?

'Keep Island Line in Franchise'

'Former Labour parliamentary candidates Stewart Blackmore and Deborah Gardiner have formed an alliance with former IW Council Conservative leader David Pugh to establish KILF – the Keep Island Line in Franchise

campaign group,' reported the *County Press* on 31 July 2015. Fearing that MP Andrew Turner's community-ownership proposal 'would inevitably result in service cuts and station closures', the new group was intending to lobby the Government, as well as holding a public meeting to which Cllr Bacon and Mr Turner would be invited, together with Mr Turner's transport advisor, Nick Finney. Similar fears about the MP's proposals were expressed at this time by the Isle of Wight Quality Transport Partnership, the Isle of Wight Bus & Rail Users' Group, and members of Sandown Town Council, although their concerns were not shared by the Chairman of Visit Isle of Wight, who 'questioned the need for the current train service connecting Ryde and Shanklin.' Mr Turner himself accused his critics of 'living in "cloud cuckoo land"'[266].

Once again the letters page of the *County Press* was dominated by Island Line, with helpful solutions from Islanders ranging from closing the line altogether to extending back to Ventnor and/or converting back to steam operation. 'Why not contact the Havenstreet railway?' suggested one correspondent.[267] In fact, the newspaper had already contacted the IWSR – which had made it very clear that it wanted nothing to do with the MP's proposal. IWSR General Manager Peter Vail stated: 'On the steam railway, we have 25 paid staff and 350 volunteers. We know that under our present structure we would not be in a position to run the community partnership … with regard to the community rail company, we most certainly would want to distance ourselves from running it.'[268] And there lay the problem. Who would want to run a loss-making railway that was reported to cost £3 million a year to operate? Clearly not the IWSR, and certainly not the cash-strapped Council either.

The KILF public meeting, which took place in Shanklin on 11 August, was attended by around 250 people who unanimously backed a resolution calling for the line to remain in the franchise. Unsurprisingly Andrew Turner MP was not present at the meeting, choosing to accept an invitation to a Cowes Week function instead. The situation was summarised by *County Press* columnist Charlotte Hofton:

'Everyone who uses the line wants the franchise option, cross-party support demands it, the council (at the time of writing, at least) wants it, the railway staff want it.

Yet the MP himself hasn't put any pressure on the government to keep Island Line in the franchise and, when given the chance to explain himself to his constituents at a large public meeting, went to a party instead.'

Ministerial letter

In early September the MP made an apparent U-turn when he told the *County Press*:

'As the timescales for Island Line are now much shorter than originally envisaged, it may well be that the Department for Transport (DfT) and ourselves agree that, for the time being, support for the Island Line comes from within the south west franchise.'[269]

Unit No 004 approaches Ryde St John's Road from the south with a Shanklin-Ryde Pier Head service on 19 June 2017. Since the closure of the signal boxes at Brading and Sandown in the late 1980s, Ryde St John's Road box, on the right, has had sole operational control of the 8½-mile line. Like the trains, the signal box was also acquired second-hand from London, having been relocated from Waterloo East in the 1920s. *Andy Sansome*

The significance of 'for the time being' became apparent the following week when rail minister Claire Perry wrote to the paper to set out the Government's current proposal for Island Line:

> 'Network Rail should take on the full cost of maintaining the line's infrastructure, including the track, pier and stations...
>
> Then, as part of the upcoming competition to run the rail network in the south west of England, the government would ask bidders to work with the Island on a plan to keep services running. That plan would need to ensure that over the next few years, the taxpayer subsidy currently paid in support of the line is reduced. That might mean securing fresh investment, or it might mean running the Island Line as a community rail scheme.'

In other words, Island Line would initially remain in the renewed franchise but probably not for the lifetime of the franchise. Stating that a formal public consultation on the proposal was going to be undertaken, Ms Perry also said that the Government would be 'supporting' the Council to set up the transport task force first suggested the previous autumn.[270] The following week saw MP and Council embroiled in a war of words as to whose fault it was that the task force hadn't been set up already.[271]

'Transport Tsar'
New developments continued throughout the autumn of 2015, with the County Press reporting in October that plans for the transport task force had been shelved and instead a 'transport tsar' appointed by the Council. Taking on this role was Christopher Garnett, an Island resident and former chief executive of GNER, who was offering his services for free. Regarding the future of Island Line, he told the paper: 'Everything is up in the air, I have got to meet with the DfT and hear where they are coming from.'[272] Despite describing himself as politically independent and happy to talk to all interested parties, Mr Garnett's appointment was immediately (and perhaps unfairly) greeted with suspicion by KILF supporters, who noted that he had once worked with the MP's transport advisor Nick Finney, albeit thirty years ago. Furthermore his appointment was described by Finney, in a letter to a railway journalist, as 'a process endorsed by Andrew Turner'[273].

The railway journalist in question was Phil Marsh, editor of The Railway Magazine, whom Mr Turner and Mr Finney succeeded in offending by first offering an interview with Finney when one had actually been requested with the MP himself, then cancelling that interview at the last minute. Speaking to the County Press, Mr Marsh stated: 'This is the first time in more than a decade of railway journalism I have been so clearly fobbed off by an MP's office and not allowed any access to an elected politician for an interview.'[274] Less than twelve months earlier Turner had been described in The Railway Magazine as 'pro-railway'[275], but unsurprisingly the magazine now turned against him and his advisor with

a full-page article pointing out that Island Line's punctuality and reliability figures – at 99.3% and 99.7% respectively – were still the best in the country and that 'the MP's proposals and lobbying could lead to the UK's most reliable branch line leaving the franchise system in April 2017, to be run locally.' Mr Turner's failure to attend the KILF debate, or any public debate on the issue, was highlighted, as was his February meeting with the rail minister at which, so a Freedom of Information request had revealed, 'a relaxation of public railway regulation and safety standards as well as transferring the line to a Social Enterprise Company (SEC)' had been discussed. The magazine pointed out that a similar SEC set up to run two lines in 2006 had pulled out within two years. The IWSR's unwillingness to consider taking over the Ryde-Shanklin line was again stated ('We see the only solution for Island Line is to stay within the franchise') while also revealed was the fact that Mr Turner had met with SWT as long ago as May 2014 to discuss possible closure of the line.[276]

Consultation
On 12 November 2015 the Department for Transport launched a consultation document on the future of the South Western franchise. The Ryde-Shanklin line, which was now stated to cost £4 million a year to operate, received special attention, with one of the key objectives for the new franchise being 'to secure an appropriate, sustainable long-term future for the Island Line'.[277] The new franchise holder would be expected to work with the Island's Council and community towards turning the line into a separate self-sustaining business during the lifetime of the franchise. Rail users now had a twelve-week period in which to respond to the consultation via post or e-mail, or by attending one of a series of public meetings that were staged by the DfT across the region. In the case of the Isle of Wight a meeting was held in Ryde during December and attended by around 150 Islanders – which the County Press was told was 'the biggest meeting by far at a southern consultation'. Attendees were told by the franchise competition's project director that 'no decision' had yet been taken regarding the future of Island Line and that 'Nothing is fixed'[278]. Meanwhile the Isle of Wight Council had commissioned two reports into the future of the line.

Atkins Report
In the autumn of 2015 a 39-page report commissioned from consultancy firm Atkins was released and proved to be somewhat controversial since it cost £20,000 of public money[279] and did little more than provide a brief overview of the current situation. Throughout the report Island Line's financial performance was unfairly compared to that of other whole franchises, rather than individual branch lines, while the conclusion simply offered five alternative options ranging from remaining in the current franchise to becoming a self-sustaining business. Attention now turned to a more comprehensive report, which had already been commissioned, for free, from the Council's own transport advisor Christopher Garnett.

Garnett Report

Having consulted a wide range of stakeholders, including town and parish councils, trade unions, the ferry companies, Southern Vectis, the IWSR, KILF and the MP himself, Christopher Garnett's report was published in February 2016. In it Garnett argues that 'There does not appear to be any clear logical arguments for Island Line being part of a wider South Western Franchise'; however, 'Island Line must stay part of the National Rail Network for ticketing, revenue allocation, information and other relevant services.'[280] Stating that the Isle of Wight Council 'would not have either the financial resources or skills' to operate the line, the report makes it clear that the line would need to remain a DfT franchise whether part of a wider franchise or not. Echoing the concerns of the 1960s, Garnett states that any attempt to close the line 'would inevitably place additional burden on a part of the Island's road network which is already working at or near capacity.'

Stating that running costs were now said to be £4.5 million per annum, in return for around £1 million revenue, Garnett expresses the view that neither a new franchise holder, nor the Isle of Wight Council, would be able to operate the line 'under the present structure and arrangements' for significantly less than SWT was already achieving. Moreover, 'given the economics of the line no private sector company would invest in the line other than through a franchise with some sort of Government support.' According to the report, the most suitable like-for-like replacements for the current tube stock would be the 1972 Stock in use on the Bakerloo Line, 'but these will not be available until 2027 at the earliest when the existing stock would be 89 years old!' Piccadilly Line stock would be available sooner, but the increased length of the coaches would create problems at Ryde Esplanade. In any case, argues the report, acquiring more tube trains would simply mean 'the continuation of the Island as it is today… The basic financial structure would be the same and it is unlikely that the total cost of the railway will be reduced.' Instead Garnett offered an alternative solution: conversion to light rail operation.

Garnett's proposal was as follows:

- The line should be improved to meet tram requirements rather than existing Network Rail standards (this would include a simplified signalling system with the trams running on line of sight).
- The track should be singled between Smallbrook Junction and Ryde St John's Road, and between Ryde St John's Road and Ryde Pier Head (whilst still retaining access to both platforms at the Pier Head itself).
- Platforms at Ryde Esplanade to be built out so that passengers can alight/join the tram from both sides – facilitating direct access to the hovercraft terminal on the seaward side of the station.
- Provision of a new passing loop at or near Brading to enable a 30-minute-interval service, with possible provision of another loop between Smallbrook Junction and Ryde St John's Road to allow a 15-minute-interval service.

- Transfer of the redundant up line between Smallbrook Junction and Ryde St John's Road to the IWSR.
- Certain engineering duties (including laying of the passing loop at Brading) to be carried out by the IWSR via a junction at Ryde St John's Road.

To operate the proposed tramway Garnett revealed: 'We have been offered the T69 tram at a very reasonable price.' These were the then recently withdrawn light rail vehicles that had operated the Midland Metro system since its inception in 1999. Having been internally refurbished in 2013, Garnett anticipated that the fifteen-year-old vehicles could last for at least ten years on the Island. Six trams would be required to operate a 15-minute service with two operational spares and another one or two spare vehicles. No extensions to the existing route are proposed, although Garnett does note that, 'A tram system would offer the potential for expansion including "street running" if desired.'

Inevitably the age-old question arises as to whether these vehicles would actually fit through Ryde Tunnel. Noting that the old steam rolling stock was 11ft 8in high and the T69 trams were 12ft 2in, Garnett states: 'It will be necessary to ascertain that, if the track level in Ryde Tunnel is reduced to the level it was prior to the introduction of the Underground stock, trams could pass through and have enough room for the catenary.' (This seems somewhat optimistic in the opinion of this author.)

Reaction to the Garnett Report

The Garnett Report was welcomed by the IWSR's General Manager[281] and the Island's MP, who stated: 'Most people are not concerned about whether Island Line is inside or outside of the south west franchise.'[282] However, its conclusion that there was no reason for the line to remain part of a wider franchise did not meet with the approval of the Council, whose formal response to the DfT's franchise consultation stated: 'Island Line should remain as a fully integrated part of the South Western rail franchise for the entire duration of the post-2017 period.' This was despite the Council leader himself, Cllr Bacon, telling the *County Press*, 'we are all in general agreement; Island Line … might benefit from local management.' Reaction from KILF was initially positive, despite the body's earlier fears about Garnett's impartiality; David Pugh welcomed the recognition that Island Line could only survive with continued outside funding, noting that the tram proposal 'is certainly one that merits further consideration'[283]. However, Garnett's suggestion that Island Line might benefit from being removed from the South Western franchise was obviously anathema to KILF's founding principles and the protest group would soon put its weight behind an alternative report.

On 16 March 2016 the Isle of Wight Council met to discuss the Garnett Report, and also a separate report that was presented to them by Cllr Ray Broomfield, a KILF member. This was *A Technical Response to the Report: 'The Future of Island Line – Options Report'*[284] written by Mark

Brinton, an Island resident and practising railway engineer of more than forty years' experience who had gained much first-hand understanding of the Ryde-Shanklin line and its rolling stock during his former BR career.

Brinton Report

While agreeing with Garnett on some points (neither Brinton nor Garnett believed that the Council or any 'community enterprise' group could successfully operate the line), much of Brinton's response takes issue with statements made in the Garnett Report. As far as Garnett's tram proposal is concerned, Brinton notes that 'Island Line is already effectively a Light Railway' and queries whether conversion to an actual tramway would involve any actual savings at all. If Island Line were to become a tramway, Brinton suspects that the DfT would seek to remove it from the National Rail network: 'This is what has happened where railway routes have been converted to tramways as in Manchester, Birmingham and London.' Regarding the specific trams recommended by Garnett, Brinton points out that 'getting a T69 tram plus overhead wire through Ryde Tunnel and under some bridges will be a significant challenge' since the height of a T69 was almost that of a main-line vehicle even before the catenary was allowed for. Brinton highlights another apparent flaw in the earlier report, that handing over the up line between Smallbrook Junction and Ryde St John's Road to the IWSR would remove the capacity to include a new passing loop between these locations – a loop that Garnett had said would be necessary to introduce a 15-minute-interval service. As far as removal from the franchise is concerned, Brinton considers that 'Island Line operating as a separate franchise is economically not sustainable in the long term' – pointing out that the DfT's earlier decision to incorporate the line within the South Western franchise had been taken on largely economic grounds.

Brinton also notes: 'Second-hand trams may seem like a good option, but one has to ask why have the vehicles been replaced by their current owners?' One might say the same about second-hand tube vehicles, although Brinton, who was one of the Project Engineers responsible for converting the 1938 Stock for Isle of Wight use, asserts that 'Rolling stock built at that time was designed to be fully repairable with effectively an "infinite" life' and that 'the existing rolling stock could be kept operational until the end of the next franchise period (7-10 years).' Regarding the ride quality of the Island's 1938 Stock, Brinton states this to be a result of the way the line is constructed and ballasted, rather than any inherent issue with the trains, and points out that funding issues mean that the infrastructure is only maintained to a legally safe standard rather than a necessarily comfortable one. On the matter of replacement tube stock, Brinton agrees that the length of the Piccadilly Line stock would present issues at Ryde Esplanade, but notes that the 1992 Stock used on the Central and Waterloo & City Lines was built to the same length as the 1972 Stock and would only be around forty years old when it became available in circa 2032. (Of course the 1938 Stock would be rapidly approaching its first century by then!) Brinton closes his report with a third option: that of upgrading the Ryde-Shanklin line to take full-size mainland rolling stock.

Brinton's proposal is as follows:

- That conversion of the line and depot to take 'standard' main line rolling stock would cost the same (or less) than conversion for light rail operation.
- Raising platform heights to suit mainland vehicles would cost no more than lowering them to suit tram vehicles.
- Economies of scale could be achieved by procuring and maintaining vehicles as part of a larger mainland fleet, rather than relying on obsolete second-hand vehicles.
- Fewer spare vehicles would be required as maintenance cover could be supplied from the mainland fleet.
- Mainland third-rail electric vehicles would be compatible with the Island's existing electrification infrastructure (unlike trams, which would require catenary, or replacement tube trains. which would again require conversion from fourth-rail).
- Island Line services would continue to operate at 45mph.
- An interconnection with the IWSR would now be justified as the upgraded Island Line infrastructure would be compatible with IWSR vehicles. Therefore sharing of some track maintenance equipment would be a realistic option, as well as the possible use of IWSR steam trains on Island Line tracks.
- Suitable rolling stock might be available shortly in the form of cascaded Class 455 and 456 units from SWT's London services or Class 508 units from Merseyrail.

(Of course this was not the first time that ex-Merseyrail units had been suggested for the Isle of Wight, although the PEP-derived Class 508s were around 4 inches higher than the Class 503s they had replaced in the 1980s.)

Perhaps surprisingly, the Council voted to reject its own Garnett Report and instead to submit the rival Brinton Report, which had already won the backing of the Isle of Wight Bus & Rail Users Group, to the DfT. This was despite the pleas of Council leader Cllr Bacon that 'it's not for us to endorse one particular viewpoint[285]'.

DfT climbdown

On 30 June 2016 the DfT issued the Invitation To Tender (ITT) for the South Western franchise. Only two bidders were in the running, with First Group/MTR competing to take over from existing franchise holder Stagecoach. As widely anticipated, the Ryde-Shanklin line was to be included in the franchise but with the proviso that bidders should develop a plan to enable Island Line to become a self-sustaining business within the expected seven-year duration of the franchise. Needless to say, this was not welcomed by KILF, which one month later announced that it was prepared to apply for a judicial review on the grounds that the Isle of Wight was being treated unfairly compared to other loss-making branch lines.[286] Faced with the threat of legal action, the DfT climbed down with almost undue haste, agreeing within days to change the wording in the ITT from 'self-sustaining' to the rather more ambiguous 'more sustainable'. DfT claims that the whole thing had merely been a misunderstanding were quickly dismissed by KILF's legal advisor, who asserted that 'anybody who has followed the debate can be in no doubt of what the DfT has been minded to do.'[287] Reporting on the debacle, *Rail* magazine also spoke to an anonymous Stagecoach source who felt that both franchise bidders 'would be likely to retain existing rolling stock throughout the next franchise' and 'carry out only a minimum amount of track work.'[288]

Franchise awarded

With the ITT suitably reworded, the worst fears were finally allayed. In March 2017 the South Western franchise, including Island Line, was awarded to First Group/MTR, ending Stagecoach's twenty-one-year association with the route. Operating as South Western Railway (SWR), the new operator took over on 20 August 2017 and once again retained the 'Island Line' brand name first created by Network SouthEast almost thirty years before. No Isle of Wight stations or trains have been reliveried so far (even on the mainland SWR has been slow to make its presence felt), all retaining their 'heritage' colours although a new 'Island Line' logo – in the style of the parent franchise's 'South Western Railway' logo – has been devised. To date, two of the six surviving 1938 Stock units have received a large white version of the new logo along the side of each carriage. While arguably destroying the effect of the heritage LT colour scheme, this nonetheless creates a surprisingly attractive impression in its own right.

SWR consultation

In the autumn of 2017 SWR launched a consultation involving all relevant stakeholders into the future of Island Line, and how best to secure its long-term future, with the launch of a publication entitled *Developing a More Sustainable Future for Island Line*.[289] This consultation was itself a legal requirement of the franchise agreement, which had specified that a consultation should commence 'no later than 31 October' with a view to submitting a 'costed option' (sometimes called the 'priced option') to the Secretary of State 'no later than 31 May 2018'. Stating that 'Island Line is important' but 'faces a challenging future', the introduction to the report lays out the bare facts as SWR saw them:

'The trains are nearly 80 years old, providing a customer experience that cannot be described as modern. Spare parts are increasingly challenging to obtain; reliability and availability is becoming an issue.
      The infrastructure also requires investment. The tunnel floods. The stations require painting. The third-rail and power supplies need replacing. Any alternative or new trains may need infrastructure changes to operate effectively.'

Of the existing rolling stock, the document notes that 'Of the fleet of six trains, three are currently serviceable' and that health and safety issues meant that guards were no longer able to pass between carriages while in motion, making ticket checks difficult. ('Anecdotal evidence suggests that revenue could be higher if revenue protection improved.') However, since the current trains were owned by the franchise, any replacements were 'likely to incur additional costs through leasing charges'. Stations were said to have received no investment 'for some time' while the inability to run a regular 30-minute-interval service 'does not serve customer needs'.

'Key stakeholders' were listed as the Isle of Wight Council, DfT, Network Rail and SWR itself. A list of almost twenty other stakeholders named in the document to be consulted included the ferry companies, the IWSR, KILF, the CRP, Bob Seely MP (Andrew Turner's successor), and Christopher Garnett (who in July 2016 had become chair of the long-delayed transport task force[290]). These were asked to respond by 31 December 2017 to more than twenty specific questions, including:

In early 2018 unit No 006 was outshopped with large SWR-style 'Island Line' logos applied on top of its LT-style red livery. Adorning a supposedly 'heritage' livery with such a prominent new logo was obviously going to be a controversial choice, but the overall effect is not unattractive. No 006 is seen here at Brading forming the 11.49 Ryde Pier Head to Shanklin service on 7 May 2018. *Andrew Long*

By the autumn of 2018 a second unit had received the new 'Island Line' branding, as can be seen from this view of No 008 heading down Ryde Pier at high tide on 8 October 2018. Behind it, the USS *Harry S. Truman* can be seen anchored in the Solent. By the time this image was taken tube trains on the pier had been an everyday sight in Ryde for more than five decades – but for how much longer...? *Nick Doolan*

- 'The South Western franchise is currently for seven years, including for Island Line. Would you support a longer investment timeframe for Island Line specifically?'
- 'How should the current lease arrangement with Network Rail be changed when it ends in 2019 and why?'
- 'What type of rolling stock do you favour?'
- 'If future rolling stock is not heavy rail, how should the infrastructure be delivered, managed, maintained and renewed?'
- 'What improvements would you like to see to Island Line stations?'

Interestingly, stakeholders were also asked, 'What is your definition of the term "more sustainable"?', suggesting perhaps that SWR itself was unsure what exactly the DfT meant by the term. (Although, given the contradictory approaches of the Island's politicians, one has to wonder if even the DfT was clear what Islanders expected of them.)

A list of rolling stock options was provided for stakeholders to comment on, including the existing 1938 Stock, re-engineered diesel trains or battery trains, new-build trains, light rail with overhead power lines (tunnel clearance was recognised to be an issue with this scenario), or a guided bus way. In conclusion the document laid out SWR's own preferred options for the future of Island Line:

- A self-powered train that can be accommodated on the existing infrastructure. This would save the cost of replacing the existing electrical equipment, which a recent dilapidation report revealed is in a poor state, with the third-rail in need of replacement and substations in poor condition. It would also avoid the storage and air pollution concerns associated with a diesel-powered train.
- A new 25-year lease, which will allow investment to be

spread across a longer period and help attract private finance.
- An enhanced service frequency to better integrate with ferry and hovercraft connections and grow business.
- Infrastructure improvements to allow better interchange between Island Line and the Isle of Wight Steam Railway to generate revenue for both organisations.
- Better marketing and revenue protection to generate revenue.

Also among items listed for early discussion was the possible extension of the steam railway into Ryde St John's Road. The IWSR's General Manager advised *The Railway Magazine* that this was seen as a genuine opportunity, but 'we are realistic and appreciate there is a long way to go'.[291]

Costed Option

SWR's Costed Option was submitted to the DfT as required in the spring of 2018, but as yet full details have not been made public. Based on SWR's stated preferences in the consultation document, as well as items that have appeared in the press since, it seems clear that the long-desired installation of a passing loop at, or near, Brading has been recommended. No mention of reopening closed lines (such as towards Ventnor) was made in the consultation document and, while extension of the IWSR into Ryde St John's Road was mentioned, there have been no hints as to whether or not it features in the Costed Option. What has been leaked is that SWR is proposing to finally replace the 1938 Stock. But what might that replacement be? Certainly not the T69 trams once proposed by Christopher Garnett, which were mostly sent for scrap during 2018. Instead much speculation has centred upon the Class 230 units being developed by Vivarail using ex-District Line D Stock.

By 8 July 2018 the Ryde-Shanklin line had been operated by First Group/MTR for almost a year, but still tourists arriving at Ryde Pier Head were greeted by this sign, proudly displaying the 'Stagecoach Island Line' logo employed during the 'dinosaur train' era. *Martyn Hilbert*

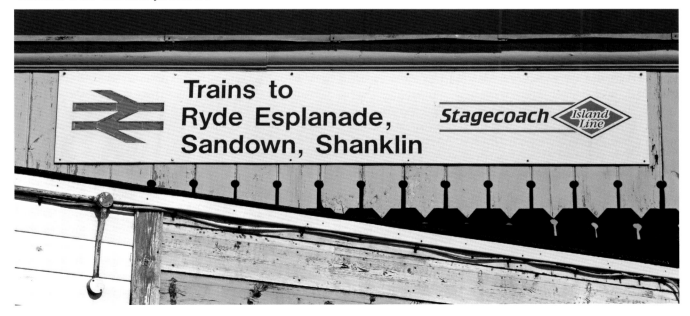

Vivarail

Vivarail was set up in 2015 by the former Chairman of Chiltern Railways, Adrian Shooter, with the intention of repurposing withdrawn London Underground District Line D78 D Stock vehicles with the intention of creating low-cost modular trains. By reusing the aluminium bodyshells, traction motors and bogies, the company has developed a new 'modular' type of train that can potentially be offered in diesel, electric or battery versions (a hydrogen version is also now in development). To date, contracts have been signed to supply diesel-powered Class 230s to West Midlands Trains and diesel-battery hybrids to Transport for Wales.

Perhaps unsurprisingly, the news that ex-London Underground trains were to be recycled led very early on to speculation that some might be destined for the Ryde-Shanklin line. As one *Railway Magazine* reader put it in December 2015, 'What better line to showcase the Vivarail D Stock trains!'[292] Undoubtedly at least some of this speculation simply arose from people making the obvious connection between old tube trains and the Isle of Wight. But of course while the District Line may be an Underground line, it is not technically a 'tube' line, having been built, like all of the earliest London Underground lines, for operation by full-size steam trains. Consequently its trains are much the same size as any other main-line UK rolling stock, something that other commentators were quick to point out. (The author must confess to having been initially sceptical himself as to the suitability of D Stock vehicles.) However, over time it became clear that maybe the Vivarail Class 230 units *were* a serious contender for the Isle of Wight after all.

In the autumn of 2017 the list of replacement rolling stock options in SWR's consultation document included 'New or re-engineered self-propelled diesel trains' and 'New or re-engineered self-propelled battery trains', with a preference being expressed for 'A self-powered train'. 'Self-powered' may be a rather ambiguous description, but the document makes it clear that neither diesel nor electric trains were being referred to, leading many to conclude that it was Vivarail-style battery trains. Further confirmation that Class 230s were under consideration seemed to come in early 2018 when the General Manager of the IWSR revealed that he had recently accepted an invitation to visit Vivarail's Long Marston headquarters to view and ride on a battery-powered unit. Noting that Class 230s were 'a possible front-runner' of the options being considered by SWR, he stated that, as far as the steam railway was concerned, 'We see them as an option for Island Line.'

But would an ex-District Line train fit the Island's restricted loading gauge, and in particular the confines of Ryde Tunnel? In 1983 it had been proposed that the track through the tunnel would need to be singled and, in parts, lowered in order to permit the use of Class 503 units. D Stock carriages are narrower than those of a Class 503 but they are also longer. In fact, at more than 59 feet a D Stock carriage remains the longest to have operated on the London Underground, and surely longer than any

to have yet operated on the Isle of Wight. D Stock carriages are also higher than a Class 503 (although at 11ft 11in the height is not dissimilar to a cut-down Class 03). Probably some overbridges might need attending to (particularly Rink Road Bridge), and certainly platform heights would need adjusting at most or all stations since, other than Ryde St John's Road, Brading and Sandown, all have been built or rebuilt since 1967 at an appropriate level for tube trains. But what of Ryde Tunnel itself? In February 2018 this author asked Vivarail, via Twitter, whether existing clearances would be generous enough or if the track floor would need to be lowered, and received the reply: 'We believe the train will fit without any changes needed at all.'

Incidentally, this author has seen it suggested in online forums that clearances within Ryde Tunnel may have been improved when, in March 2006, a section of the Victorian tunnel roof built of wrought iron was removed and replaced with eighteen concrete beams and six steel beams. There *may* be some truth in this assertion, although if clearances were improved no mention of it was made at the time in the coverage that appeared in both the *County Press* and *Island Rail News*. In any case it should be noted that changes to the roof would make no difference to the restrictive curvature of the tunnel and that only one section of tunnel roof was replaced while the brick-arched construction that covers the bulk of the tunnel remains as built.

Speaking to *Rail* magazine in July 2018, Vivarail Chairman Adrian Shooter 'declined to comment on speculation' that Class 230s might be destined for the Isle of Wight[293]; however, the October issue of *Modern Railways* reported:

'Mr Shooter confirms that the Class 230s will fit through the tunnel at Ryde... He explains that all Class 230s built so far have included 45mm of packing to lift the trains, but units built for the Island Line would not include this.'

The same article also confirms:

'Introduction of Class 230s on the Island Line service between Ryde and Shanklin is South Western Railway operator FirstGroup's preferred solution for the line ... but a formal deal is subject to confirmation from the Department for Transport, with a decision expected by the end of the year.'[294]

In fact, no such decision was forthcoming by the end of 2018, with the February 2019 edition of *The Railway Magazine* confirming instead that the DfT had deferred its decision on SWR's Costed Option until the end of March, before also stating that 'it seems Vivarail may be providing trains to replace the 1938 Stock.'[295] 'Coincidentally,' noted the magazine, the end of March 2019 would also mark the expiry of the original twenty-five-year lease on the Island Line's infrastructure.

'Island Line'-branded No 006 emerges from the southern portal of Ryde Tunnel as the 13.49 Ryde Pier Head to Shanklin service on 12 July 2018. *Martyn Hilbert*

Lease expiration

The expiry of the original twenty-five-year lease, and what that might mean for the future maintenance of Island Line's infrastructure, has generated much less attention than the possible replacement of its tube trains. But arguably it is of even greater significance, for without a maintained infrastructure there is no railway for the trains to run on. In 2015 the then rail minister, Claire Perry, advised the *County Press* that 'the Government's proposal is that Network Rail should take on the full cost of maintaining the line's infrastructure, including the track, pier and stations'[296] – in other words, that the lease should not be renewed and that Network Rail should take full responsibility for infrastructure as everywhere else on the national network. However, only one year later the paper reported that the DfT 'has now said it would be premature to decide on funding, stating it would be up to the next franchisee to come up with a long-term plan.' This apparent u-turn prompted fears from KILF that 'the next franchisee could well choose to avoid the significant cost of upgrading the pier by truncating services at the Esplanade.'[297] The 'long-term plan' that the Government expected the next franchisee to come up with would of course take the form of SWR's consultation document and

subsequent Costed Option. In the former SWR expressed the view that 'the most appropriate way forward' would be 'a new 25-year lease which will allow investment to be spread across a longer period'. The same document also made it clear that 'Ryde Pier is Network Rail's responsibility to maintain rather than the franchisee.' For this reason the Costed Option itself evidently did not contain proposals for the future maintenance of the railway pier, which had seen no major maintenance since the rebuild of the 1960s. A letter written by the Island's MP, Bob Seely, to the transport minister in November 2018 in support of SWR's proposals ('We are not seeking new, bespoke rail vehicles, but instead reconditioned rolling stock from the 1970s') ends with the plea, 'I would seek your assurance of the Government's commitment – through Network Rail – to make the necessary investment in Ryde Pier.'[298]

The DfT may have failed to make a decision on the Costed Option by the end of 2018, but it did at least make one decision. Following a meeting with Mr Seely shortly before Christmas the transport minister announced:

'We expect Network Rail to be making provision for, and planning to undertake, all necessary work required to maintain the Island Line train service in accordance with its asset management responsibilities. For the avoidance of doubt, that includes the Ryde Pier railway.'[299]

Whether the line will continue to retain its unique 'vertical' structure for the foreseeable future (as seems to be SWR's preferred option) or whether Network Rail will assume full responsibility for infrastructure maintenance remains unclear at the time of writing, but the future of Ryde's railway pier does at least appear to be assured.

Decision delayed?

As of May 2019 the long-delayed decision on the future of Island Line has still to be announced by the Department for Transport. (To be fair, the Government may have been a little preoccupied with other, Brexit-related, matters.) Quite possibly the situation will have been resolved by the time this book is published, but in the meantime the lack of an announcement makes the future a little hard to predict, although what can be said is that the vexed issue of the infrastructure lease, which had been due to expire on 31 March 2019, does appear to have been temporarily resolved. Posting on the KILF Facebook page on 13 April David Pugh revealed that members of the Island Line Stakeholder Forum had been informed that "A short-term extension has been given to the existing lease whilst the new one is finalised".

One possible glimpse of the future did raise its head in the March 2019 edition of *Steam Railway* magazine, with a prediction that 'The Isle of Wight Steam Railway could finally realise its long-held dream of reconnecting with Ryde in 2021.'[300] Discussions are said to be 'at an early stage' between the IWSR, SWR and the Office of Rail & Road, and a number of possible options are laid out, all of them involving the IWSR having exclusive use of the existing up line between Smallbrook and Ryde St John's Road – although in each scenario Island Line is expected to continue to use Ryde St John's Platform 1 itself. (All options involve either shared use of Platform 1 or else a new IWSR platform being constructed to the south of the existing station). No mention is made in the article of the expected DfT decision, although some outcomes of that decision are clearly anticipated, specifically that Island Line will be resignalled 'in winter 2020/21', that this will involve the installation of a passing loop at Brading, and that the existing up line between Smallbrook and Ryde St John's Road will become redundant. No mention is made of replacement Island Line rolling stock, although interestingly an assumption is made that third-rail electrification will still be present at Ryde St John's.

The fate of the 1938 stock

And what of the Island's 1938 Stock? After more than five decades it seems that the Isle of Wight's remarkable association with tube trains is finally coming to a close, even if, ironically, they seem likely to be replaced with yet another fleet of ex-London Underground vehicles. All six of the two-car 1938 Stock sets that passed to Stagecoach

Unit No 004 makes its way up Ryde Pier at high tide on 2 July 2017 with the 17.18 service from Shanklin while the cruise liner *Celebrity Eclipse* is visible on the horizon. Having entered LT service in October 1939, No 004 is the oldest train in service on the National Rail network. In recent years the unit has been easily recognisable by the poor condition of the paintwork on its roof. *Martyn Hilbert*

Unit No 004 makes a striking sight as it approaches Lake as the 10.49 Ryde Pier Head to Shanklin service on 7 July 2017. The mural under the pedestrian subway commemorates the famous 'Eight Wonders of the Isle of Wight' – including 'Lake where there is no water'. *Martyn Hilbert*

on the Island's privatisation remain extant. One set, No 002, has been out of service for many years (uniquely it still retains its 'Raptor' name from the dinosaur period) and is currently being stripped for spares. Consisting of cars Nos 122 and 225 (the latter originally from scrapped unit No 005), unit No 002 is the only hybrid formation of the surviving fleet. The other five sets (Nos 004 and 006-009) are all nominally serviceable although in reality only three or four sets are ever in a serviceable condition at a time. A minimum of two sets is required two operate a two-trains-per-hour service, and recently it has not been unheard of for the failure of a single unit to cause the service to be temporarily reduced to just hourly. Observations suggest that no four-car sets have run for several years. All vehicles are now around eighty years old, considerably older than their Standard Stock predecessors were on withdrawal, and older even than the 'O2' tanks were on their withdrawal in the 1960s. (The age of the tube cars led to an unexpected publicity story for the IWSR in 2016 when an Island Line train failed at Smallbrook Junction only for its passengers to be rescued by a steam train hauled by a 'modern' Ivatt locomotive built as recently as 1951![301]) By comparison, in mainland Britain the oldest non-heritage passenger rail vehicles still in regular usage were built in the 1970s.

When the time comes, does preservation beckon for any of the tube cars or will they face the same fate as almost all of their Standard Stock predecessors? It seems unlikely this time that any will return to London since the London Transport Museum already has an operational four-car 'heritage' 1938 Stock set, together with a fifth such vehicle on display at Covent Garden. On the Island itself, if SWR is planning to remove the third-rail and de-electrify the line, there will be no opportunity for a preserved tube train to operate under its own power between Ryde and Shanklin – but there are hopes that one vehicle (or part of one) might this time end up at Havenstreet. According to the IWSR's Strategic Vision document:

'When the tube stock is taken out of service we will secure a representative example of the current Island Line stock for static museum display. This may not be a complete vehicle, but could be a representative part of a vehicle imaginatively displayed.'[302]

Whatever happens it seems that soon, like the steam trains and trams before them, the final tube train will rattle its way down Ryde Pier and into history. No doubt people will one day look back on them as nostalgically as they now remember their predecessors.

Appendix: The Class 503 Proposal

Memorandum dated 25 April 1983, sent by British Rail's Isle of Wight Manager to the Area Manager, Portsmouth.

British Rail   BR 4/2

to Area Manager,   from Manager,
   PORTSMOUTH.   Isle of Wight,
                                           RYDE ST JOHNS ROAD.
                                      ext. 089-8822

                                      y/r   o/r M/503
                                      date   date 25 April 1983.

ISLE OF WIGHT RAILWAY ROLLING STOCK.

1. **INTRODUCTION**

    In recent months there has been a marked increase of failures in traffic, (Appendix A), which is causing widespread concern about the poor condition of the present Isle of Wight rolling stock. In addition it should be noted that there have been a number of 'wrong side' electrical failures, such as the 'doors closed' indicator being illuminated with a door still open.

2. **CONDITION OF ISLE OF WIGHT STOCK.**

    The failures listed in Appendix A do not include units that have remained in service with defects awaiting attention such as, doors isolated, defective heaters, defective lights, defective Guard's panels etc., or faults that have been rectified in traffic. In addition units are often restricted to working on Ryde Pier only, either as a result of defects or because they are overdue for mileage exam.

    2.1. Refurbishing Programme.

    In connection with the current programme of refurbishing it must be understood that this is little more than a cosmetic exercise which has failed to cure the following faults : -

    2.1.1. Doors : - Many of the sliding doors do not work properly and the rubber seals are perished and inefective. This creates draughts and allows rainwater to enter the interior. In the case of the hinged doors many are difficult to open and close, which is dangerous for the staff involved.

    2.1.2. Windows : - A large number of windows fit badly and in consequence rainwater enters the passenger compartments, soaking the new upholstery and rotting the woodwork.

    2.1.3. Repainting : - Where the paint has been applied over rotten timber it is already peeling off.

    2.1.4. Driving Cabs : - Rainwater continues to enter the driving cabs and there has been little reduction in draughts. This matter was raised previously in correspondance and an assurance given that the situation would be improved.

3.   <u>CARRIAGE CLEANING</u>.

Due to the limited siding accomodation at Ryde St Johns Road, together with the fact that all exterior cleaning is carried out in the Down Platform Siding, it is essential that the units maintain a regular rotation to ensure adequate cleaning. The rising failure rate has meant an increase in the number of units 'stopped' by the CM&EE and in consequence it has not been possible to carry out a regular programme of carriage cleaning. This is an extremely worrying situation, particularly as the Isle of Wight County Council has made a financial contribution to the cost of the current refurbishing programme.

4.   <u>ROLLING STOCK REPLACEMENT</u>.

The foregoing is not intended as a critiscism of the local CM&EE staff, who are no doubt doing their best in difficult circumstances, but rather to draw attention to the unacceptable condition of the present rolling stock.

Consideration should also be given to Sealink's plans to introduce new ferries and terminal facilities on the Portsmouth - Ryde route which, by comparison, will make the present units appear more decrepit than ever.

Thus, in view of the deteriorating condition of the existing stock it will be necessary to give urgent consideration to finding suitable replacements and to this end there would appear to be two main options.

4.1.   London Transport Underground Stock.

It is not anticipated that L.T. will dispose of any stock suitable for use on the Island before 1990 which, in the present situation, will not be soon enough. The main advantage of using former L.T. stock is that it conforms to the restricted loading gauge applicable to the Isle of Wight. However, in addition to the current non availability such stock has a number of disadvantages : -

4.1.1.   Conversion Costs : - Underground stock requires electrical conversion for use on Third Rail electrified lines. Other costs, assuming a similar situation to that applicable to the present units, include turning of all wheelsets to the correct profile and the provision of additional luggage space.

4.1.2.   Spares and Maintainance : - It will be necessary to continue to obtain spare parts from L.T. and to arrange for the overhaul of components at L.T. workshops.

4.1.3.   Capacity : - The present units have a limited capacity which often involves the operation of relief services and the provision of additional trains between Ryde Pier Head and the Esplanade.

4.1.4.   Suitability : - It has become apparent that many of the present faults can be traced to the continuous use of deep level tube stock in an open air environment.

4.2.   Class 503 'Merseyrail' Units.

The transfer of the 508 stock to Merseyside will result in withdrawal of the Class 503 electric units at present in use on the Wirral lines of the Liverpool Division. These units, details of which are included in Appendix B, would be ideally suited to the Isle of Wight. A comparison between the Class 503 and the present stock is given in Appendix C. The main advantages of the 503 stock are as follows : -

4.2.1.   Availability : - The units would become available in 1983/4 and would require no modification in order to work on the Island.

4.2.2.   Capacity : - Because of the increased capacity of this stock it would be possible for the service to be operated by 9 three car units (27 vehicles) instead of the present 5 seven car sets and two spare vehicles (37 vehicles) a reduction of 27%.

4.2.3.   Operating Economies : - The use of three and six car formations would result in a considerable saving in vehicle mileage, maintainance, (motor coaches would be reduced from 16 to 9), and traction current requirements. In addition some services on Ryde Pier could be withdrawn.

4.2.4.   Guards Vans : - 503 units are equipped with vans and this would permit the carriage of bicycles, luggage, parcels etc., all of which will provide an increase in revenue. Also, if all vans are marshalled at the Ryde End of trains, Guards would be able to issue and collect tickets at Ryde St Johns Road, Brading and the proposed station at Lake, with a consequential increase in revenue.

4.2.5.   Platform Maintainance : - The operation of six car trains would enable platform lengths to be reduced at Ryde Pier Head and Ryde Esplanade. In both cases the platform ends are of timber construction, in poor condition and in need of replacement. The reduced train length would also give a reduction in the construction costs of the proposed station at Lake.

5.   STRUCTURAL ALTERATIONS.

Replacement of the existing stock, by either former L.T. Underground trains or Class 503 units, will entail alterations to the inspection pit facilities in the CM&EE maintainance depot at Ryde St Johns Road. Such modifications being necessary in order to provide access to underfloor mounted equipment.

In the case of 503 stock a short extension of covered accomodation on No 3 road would enable a three car unit to be serviced without the need for intermediate shunting. This reduction of 'down time' would permit quicker and more efficient servicing which in turn would enable more time to be spent on carrying out any necessary repair work.

5.1.   Ryde Tunnel.

This structure, consisting of both single and double line

bores, has a very restricted clearance. Preliminary
investigation indicates that alterations would be required in
order to accomodate the class 503 units. The cheapest option,
made possible by recent reductions in train service levels,
would be to single the line between Ryde St Johns Road and
Ryde Esplanade. The remaining line through the tunnel could
then be lowered in the single track bores, either by
excavation or the use of slab paved track, and slewed to the
centre of the present double line section.

The reduction of this section to single track would
enable the very sharp curves that exist at present to be
eased, reducing maintainance costs and permitting the present
20m.p.h. permanent speed restriction to be raised.

Details of the proposed track and signalling alterations
are given in Appendix D.

5.2.   Station Platforms.

The introduction of Class 503 stock might make it necessary
to slightly raise the height of the platforms at Ryde Pier
Head and Ryde Esplanade. The platforms at other Island
Stations were not lowered to accomodate the present L.T.
stock.

6.   HIGH SEAS : RYDE PIER.

During periods of high seas it is necessary to terminate trains
at Ryde Esplanade and withdraw the service on Ryde Pier. At present
such a situation arises approximately three times a year. It has
been stated that the use of units with underfloor equipment would
require the service to be withdrawn more frequently. However, this
is unlikely to be the case, particularly with class 503 units which
are higher off the ground than L.T. Stock.

It should be noted that at the present time it is short
circuiting of the traction current, not damage to the rolling stock,
that necessitates suspension of services.

7.   CONCLUSION

It is clear that the question of replacing the present Island
Stock must be considered as a matter of urgency. With regard to the
availability of suitable stock it would appear that the class 503
'Merseyrail' units are ideally suited for use on the Isle of Wight.

In view of the fact that these units once delivered to the
Island, would be isolated from main works attention, they should be
given a C1 general overhaul before leaving the mainland. At the
same time they could be repainted in the distinctive Isle of Wight
livery in use on the present stock.

Finally, there is a strong probability that the present Isle
of Wight County Council (which has a further two years in office)
would be prepared to contribute to the cost of the structural
alterations necessary to accomodate the class 503 stock.

ISLE OF WIGHT RAILWAY ROLLING STOCK : FAILURES IN TRAFFIC.

Date	Train	Unit	Defect
6/1/83	07 15	043	Electrical. Unit taken out of Service.
9/1/83		041/D	Brakes failing to release.
12/1/83		032/D	Connecting Door will not open. Guards floor panels rotten and lifting up.
23/1/83		043/A	Downside doors would not open on S5 and the adjacent trailer. Once opened the doors then opened and closed on their own.
28/1/83	14 07	034	Hot Axle Box. Unit taken out of Service.
31/1/83		044/D	Wooden frame of cab centre door rotten, causing draughts and allowing rainwater to enter the cab.
7/2/83		043/D	Upside Guards door will not open or close.
9/2/83		041/D	Downside Guards door will not open or close.
11/2/83	07 38	S10/031	Electrical. Unit taken out of Service.
12/2/83	09 37	041	Overdue Mileage Exam. Unit taken out of Service.
12/2/83	14 37		Lighting fault. Unit taken out of Service.
14/2/83	10 07	045	Electrical. Unit taken out of Service.
15/2/83		042/S22	Hole in floor under downside driving cab door, leaking in wet weather.
17/2/83	17 07	031	Failed at Ryde St Johns Road, loss of power.
18/2/83		044/A	Intermittent audible warning.
22/2/83		041	No weak field.
23/2/83		041/S13	Driving Cab centre door leaking rainwater.
24/2/83		041/A	Downside lighting switch defective.
25/2/83		044/S4	Holes in Guards floor, wood and steel rotten.
25/2/83		041/A	Downside lighting switch defective.
26/2/83		044/S4	Rubber seal on Guards door defective.

Date	Train	Unit	Defect
2/3/83	18 16	041	Defective Guards door. Unit taken out of Service.
3/3/83	07†50	042	Defective Brakes. Unit taken out of Service.
8/3/83		035/S10	Door closed Indicator illuminated with doors still open.
11/3/83		032/D	Up side doors isolated from Guards Panel without Guards key inserted.
15/3/83	09 07	041	Electrical. Unit taken out of Service.
16/3/83		045/D	Defective heater in Driving Cab.
17/3/83		045/S6	No signal light or starting bell.
19/3/83	07 15	034/042	Defective Brakes. Unit taken out of Service.
21/3/83		041/A	Guards door electrical interlocking defective. No signal light from D End.
23/3/83	08 11	032	Overdue mileage exam. Unit taken out of Service.
23/3/83	10 07	043	Overdue mileage exam. Unit taken out of Service.
24/3/83	06 20	042	Electrical. Unit taken out of Service.
24/3/83	09 03	032	Electrical. Unit taken out of Service.
24/3/83	10 37	041	Overdue mileage exam. Unit taken out of Service.
26/3/83		045/A	Guards door bar defective.
27/3/83		041/s27	Defective lighting.
27/3/83		045	Defective signal light and starting bells.
1/4/83	12 07	045/035	Defective control gear. Unit taken out of Service, 12 07 & 12 30 services cancelled.
1/4/83		041/D	Brakes failing to release.
2/4/83		045/D	Door closed indicator illuminated with doors still open.
2/4/83		041/D	Brakes failing to release.
6/4/83	07 27		Defective Brakes. 3-Set taken out of Service.

Date	Train	Unit	Defect
7/4/83		041/A	Defective signal light and Guards door.
10/4/83		032	Defective signal lights and starting bells.
11/4/83		045/S9	Guards upside door defective.
11/4/83		041/S20	Guards panel defective, doors will not shut.
15/4/83	07 27	034/045	Electrical. Unit taken out of Service.
18/4/83	07 15	031	Defective signal light and starting bells, Unit taken out of Service.
18/4/83	15 37	034	Defective doors. Unit taken out of Service, 15 37 & 16 11 services cancelled.
18/4/83	16 07	043	Defective control gear. Unit taken out of Service.
24/4/83	08 17	045/035	Defective traction motors. Unit taken out of Service.

Diesel Locomotive 97803

Date			Defect
9/4/83			Locomotive failed to start. Engineering Works cancelled.
16/4/83			Passing Smallbrook the cab filled with fumes, and difficulty was experienced with the clutch and gearbox. Locomotive returned to Ryde and Engineering works cancelled.
23/4/83			Following a test run on 22/4/83 CM&EE confirmed loco a failure until further notice. Drivers training course for week commencing 3rd May 1983 cancelled. (Previously cancelled due to earlier failure of locomotive).

APPENDIX B

CLASS 503 UNITS (1956 BUILD).

BUILT   1956

BUILDER   Metropolitan Cammell and Birmingham Railway
                         Carriage and Wagon Company.

ELECTRICAL EQUIPMENT   Metropolitan Vickers.

BRAKES   Westinghouse Electro-Pneumatic.

TRACTION CURRENT   650v DC Third Rail.

TRACTION MOTORS   4 x 135 H.P.

MOTOR RATING   135 H.P. 1 Hour.
                          93 H.P. Continuous.

UNIT FORMATION   MOTOR OPEN BRAKE SECOND (MOB)

                         Dimensions   58' x 8'8'' x 9'11''
                         Weight   36 Tons
                         Traction Motors 4 x 135 H.P. B.T.H.
                         Seats   58
                         Coach Numbers   M28371M - M28394M Inclusive.

                         TRAILER OPEN SECOND (TOS) (Formerly Composite)

                         Dimensions   56' x 8'8'' x 9'11''
                         Weight   21 Tons
                         Seats   55 (40/15)
                         Coach Numbers   M29821M - M29846M Inclusive.

                         DRIVING TRAILER OPEN SECOND (DTO)

                         Dimensions   58' x 8'8'' x 9'11''
                         Weight   21 Tons
                         Seats   68
                         Coach Numbers   M29131M - M29156M Inclusive.

APPENDIX C

COMPARISON BETWEEN CLASS 503 AND CLASS 485/486.

	503 (3-Set)	4-Veo (4-Set)
TRACTION CURRENT	650v DC	630v DC
TRACTION MOTORS	4 x 135 H.P.	4 x 240 H.P.
	540 H.P.	960 H.P.
LENGTH	172'	207'11½''
WIDTH	8'8''	8'8½''
WEIGHT	78 Tons	96 Tons
SEATS	184	132
WEIGHT PER SEAT	0.43 Tons	0.73 Tons

	2 x 503 (6-Set)	4-Veo/3-Tis (7-Set)
TRACTION MOTORS	8 x 135 H.P.	6 x 240 H.P.
	1080 H.P.	1440 H.P.
LENGTH	344'	363'
WEIGHT	156 Tons	163 Tons
SEATS	362	236

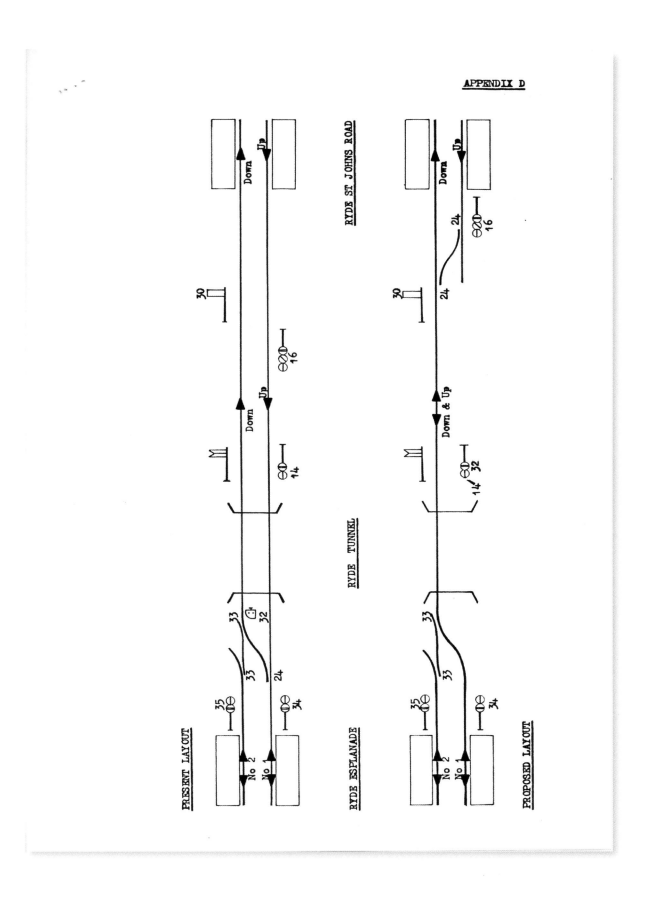

Notes

Chapter One

[1] *Isle of Wight County Press*, 'Island Railways: Probable Life of Ten Years' (24 October 1953), p7

[2] *The Times*, 'Beeching Report Proposes Closing Nearly a Third of Britain's 7,000 Railway Stations' (28 March 1963), p8

[3] *Isle of Wight County Press*, 'Closure of Railways This Year Has Been Averted' (6 April 1963), p11

[4] *Isle of Wight County Press*, 'Higher Fares, Less Comfort' (7 October 1961), p7

[5] *Isle of Wight County Press*, 'All Aboard for the Daffodil Line!' (2 February 1963), p6

[6] *Isle of Wight County Press*, 'No Room for Sentiment Over Railways' (9 February 1963), p8

[7] Ibid

[8] *Isle of Wight County Press*, 'Future of Island's Transport is in Private Enterprise' (26 September 1953), p8

[9] *Isle of Wight County Press*, 'Death Knell of Bennie Airspeed Railway' (21 November 1953), p7

[10] *Isle of Wight County Press*, 'Dr Beeching and Island Railways' (6 April 1963), p10

[11] *Isle of Wight County Press*, 'Island Highways' (24 November 1962), p10

[12] *Isle of Wight County Press*, 'No Room for Sentiment Over Railways' (9 February 1963), p8

[13] *Isle of Wight County Press*, 'Island Highways' (24 November 1962), p10

[14] *Isle of Wight County Press*, 'Dr Beeching and Island Railways' (6 April 1963), p10

[15] *Isle of Wight County Press*, 'Future of Railways Still Undecided' (20 January 1962), p7

[16] *Isle of Wight County Press*, 'Local Summary' (2 March 1907), p5

[17] *Isle of Wight County Press*, 'N.U.R. in Fight to Save Railway' (22 June 1963), p11

[18] Ibid

[19] *Isle of Wight County Press*, 'Island Member and Buses' (6 April 1963), p16

[20] *Isle of Wight County Press*, 'The Fight Ahead' (30 March 1963), p8

[21] Ibid

[22] *Isle of Wight County Press*, '"Do Not Panic Over the Railway"' (6 April 1963), p7

[23] *Isle of Wight County Press*, 'N.U.R. in Fight to Save Railway' (22 June 1963), p11

[24] *Isle of Wight County Press*, 'British Railways Explain the Beeching Proposals' (1 June 1963), p9

[25] *Isle of Wight County Press*, 'Ryde Pier Head May Become a Bus Station' (17 August 1963), p9

[26] *Isle of Wight County Press*, 'British Railways To Hold Staff Consultation Meeting' (25 January 1964), p9

[27] *The Railway Magazine*, 'Tube Trains on Ryde Pier' (April 1964), p388

[28] *Isle of Wight County Press*, 'Withdrawal of Railway Passenger Services' (22 February 1964), p10

[29] *Isle of Wight County Press*, '"Severe Hardship" If Ryde-Ventnor Line Closes' (13 June 1964), pp13-14

[30] *Isle of Wight County Press*, 'British Railways Buy Underground Trains' (22 August 1964), p11

[31] *Isle of Wight County Press*, 'Railway Decision Soon' (19 December 1964), p9

[32] R. E. Burroughs, *The Great Isle of Wight Train Robbery* (1968), p22

[33] B. Hardy, *Tube Trains on the Isle of Wight* (2003), p12

[34] *The Times*, 'Nine Stations to Close on I.O.W.' (29 July 1965), p7

[35] *Isle of Wight County Press*, 'Ryde-Shanklin Railway to Continue' (31 July 1965), p11

[36] *Isle of Wight County Press*, 'Hovercraft Service Opens at Cowes' (9 July 1966), p15

Chapter Two

[37] *Isle of Wight County Press*, 'Rail Closure – "A Matter of Weeks"' (15 January 1966), p9

[38] B. Hardy, *Tube Trains on the Isle of Wight* (2003), p10

[39] The Ryde-Shanklin line is often reported to have been electrified at 630 volts DC, although in his 2016 report rail engineer Mark Brinton (see Chapter 8) dismisses this figure as a 'myth' perpetuated by enthusiast books, saying: 'The Island Line 3 rail system has always operated in excess of 700 volts.'

[40] *Isle of Wight County Press*, 'Rail Modernisation Costs' (12 February 1966), p9

[41] *The Times*, 'Visiting Admiralty Judge' (2 July 1966), p7

[42] *Isle of Wight County Press*, 'Isle of Wight Railway Electrification' (2 July 1966), p11

[43] Full details of all tube vehicles reserved for, or transferred to, the Isle of Wight can be found in the book *Tube Trains on the Isle of Wight* by Brian Hardy (2003)

[44] *Isle of Wight County Press*, 'Electric Rail Coach Has No Mail Van' (10 September 1966), p11

[45] *Isle of Wight County Press*, 'Railway Electrification' (10 December 1966), p19

[46] *Isle of Wight County Press*, 'Electric Trains Show Their Paces' (4 March 1967), p10

[47] *Isle of Wight County Press*, 'Island's "Renaissant" Railway' (25 March 1967), p9

[48] *Isle of Wight County Press*, 'Second Hand Trains for the Island' (22 August 1964), p10

[49] *Isle of Wight County Press*, 'Future of Island Railways' (19 February 1966), p10
[50] *Isle of Wight County Press*, 'Island Member and the Railways' (12 March 1966), p11
[51] *Isle of Wight County Press*, 'Railway Fares' (25 March 1967), p8
[52] *Isle of Wight County Press*, 'Success of Electric Train Service' (29 July 1967), p11
[53] *Isle of Wight County Press*, 'Member Meets Young Electors' (17 January 1970), p10
[54] *Isle of Wight County Press*, 'Conservative Annual Meetings' (13 April 1963), p6
[55] *Isle of Wight County Press*, 'Ryde-Shanklin Railway to Continue' (31 July 1965), p11
[56] *Isle of Wight County Press*, 'Rail Closure Affected Ventnor Season' (3 December 1966), p11
[57] *Isle of Wight County Press*, 'Railway Electrification to Wroxall' (17 September 1966), p9
[58] *Isle of Wight County Press*, 'Moves to Re-open Shanklin-Ventnor Railway' (21 January 1967), p9
[59] *Isle of Wight County Press*, 'Island's "Renaissant" Railway' (25 March 1967), p9
[60] *Wight Report* issue 4, 'Notes & News' (Autumn 1968), p8
[61] *Isle of Wight County Press*, '"Unfortunate" Railway Decisions' (17 September 1966), p10
[62] *Wight Report* issue 16, 'Island Railway Notes & News' (Winter 1971-72), p3

Chapter Three

[63] *Isle of Wight County Press,* 'Success of Electric Train Service' (29 July 1967), p11
[64] *Wight Report* issue 3, 'Notes & News' (July 1968), p11
[65] *Wight Report* issue 5, 'The Pier Tramway Past & Present' (Winter 1969), p11
[66] Ibid
[67] A. Blackburn & J. Mackett, *The Railways and Tramways of Ryde* (1971), p142
[68] *Isle of Wight County Press*, 'Ryde Pier Trams protest' (11 January 1969), p9
[69] *Wight Report* issue 5, 'Island Railway Notes & News' (Winter 1969), p6
[70] *Isle of Wight County Press*, 'Tale of a Ryde Tram' (1 February 1969), p9
[71] *Wight Report* issue 6, 'Last Connecting Tram For Boat Has Departed' (Spring 1969), p14
[72] *Isle of Wight County Press*, 'Shanklin' (1 February 1969), p13
[73] *Isle of Wight County Press*, '"Hell-for-Leather" Rush for Trains' (26 April 1969), p6
[74] *Isle of Wight County Press*, 'Vectrail to Occupy Railway Line' (19 April 1969), p6
[75] *Isle of Wight County Press*, 'Federation of Ratepayers' Associations' (21 November 1970), p10
[76] *Isle of Wight County Press*, 'Member Meets Young Electors' (17 January 1970), p10
[77] *Isle of Wight County Press*, 'Vintage Transport Group Acquire Ryde Tram' (15 March 1969), p15
[78] *Isle of Wight County Press*, 'Ryde Pier Tram Moved to Newport' (28 February 1970), p8
[79] *Isle of Wight County Press*, 'Ryde Pier Tram in Working Order' (23 January 1971), p11
[80] *Isle of Wight County Press*, 'Popular Whitsun Attraction' (5 June 1971), p12
[81] *Isle of Wight County Press*, '"Spitfire" arrives at Centre' (17 June 1972), p13
[82] *Wight Report* issue 15, 'Island Railway Notes and News' (Autumn 1971), p5
[83] *Isle of Wight County Press*, 'Ferry slices through Ryde Pier' (10 March 1973), p17
[84] *Wight Report* issue 20, 'Island Railway Notes & News' (Spring 1973), p9
[85] R. J. Maycock & R. Silsbury: *The Piers, Tramways and Railways at Ryde* (2005), p149
[86] Car No 2 is not the only surviving ex-Ryde Tram vehicle: the so-called 'Grapes' car of 1871 is displayed in Hull's 'Streetlife' Museum, while after storage at various locations the body of one of the electric tramcars, built by Pollard & Sons in 1911, was donated to the Isle of Wight Steam Railway in 2017 and is now displayed at Havenstreet in the Train Story exhibition.

Chapter Four

[87] *Isle of Wight County Press*, 'Newport-Cowes-Railway' (23 October 1965), p11
[88] *The Railway Magazine*, 'Vectrail Developments' (November 1966), pp662-663
[89] *Isle of Wight County Press*, 'Newport-Cowes-Railway' (18 April 1970), p15
[90] *Wight Report* issue 6, 'Progress Report' (Spring 1969), p2
[91] *Isle of Wight County Press*, 'Future of Rail Transport' (4 April 1970), p10
[92] *Isle of Wight County Press*, 'Cowes-Ryde Railway Decision' (26 September 1970), p10
[93] *Wight Report* issue 11, 'Progress' (Autumn 1970), pp1-2
[94] *Isle of Wight County Press*, 'Future of Rail Transport' (7 March 1970), p14
[95] R. E. Burroughs, *The Great Isle of Wight Train Robbery* (1968), p25

[96] *Isle of Wight County Press*, 'Member Meets Young Electors' (17 January 1970), p10

[97] *The Railway Magazine*, '"Pay trains" on the Isle of Wight' (January 1970), p47

[98] *Wight Report* issue 15, 'Island Railway Notes and News' (Autumn 1971), p5

[99] *Wight Report* issue 16, 'Island Railway Notes & News' (Winter 1971-72), p4

[100] *Wight Report* issue 20, 'Island Railway Notes & News' (Spring 1973), p8

[101] *Isle of Wight County Press*, 'Hoteliers Call for More Winter Amenities' (27 December 1975), p2

[102] *Isle of Wight County Press*, 'Railway Line: Govt. Will Decide' (11 December 1976), p1

[103] *Wight Report* issue 15, 'Island Railway Notes and News' (Autumn 1971), p5

[104] *Modern Tramway and Light Rail Transit* Vol 50 No 594, 'Ryde Rail' (June 1987), pp195-196

[105] *Isle of Wight County Press*, 'B.R. asked: why neglect Island stations' (15 September 1973), p19

[106] *Wight Report* issue 14, 'Island Railway Notes & News' (Summer 1971), p7

[107] *Wight Report* issue 16, 'Island Railway Notes & News' (Winter 1971-72), p4

[108] *Wight Report* issue 15, 'Island Railway Notes and News' (Autumn 1971), p5

[109] *Isle of Wight County Press*, 'Shanklin to Lose its Relic from Age of Steam' (6 October 1979), p1

[110] *The Guardian*, 'In Newport, Isle of Wight' (25 February 1978), p17

[111] *Isle of Wight County Press*, 'IW "Cinderella" of Rail System Hoteliers Told' (24 November 1979), p33

[112] *Portsmouth Evening News*, 'Services Hit by Brading Derailment' (24 February 1981)

[113] The author has been advised that the Council had been unofficially tipped-off by the management at Ryde in advance of the 25 April proposal.

[114] *Isle of Wight County Press*, 'Carriages Get an £80,000 Facelift' (12 November 1982), p2

Chapter Five

[115] *Isle of Wight County Press*, 'Railway "Maid-of-all Work"' (15 October 1966), p11

[116] Photos of No D2554 taken at Colchester in 1960-61, several years before transfer to the Island, show it with a cab profile seemingly identical to that it retains to this day.

[117] *The Railway Magazine*, 'Locomotive News' (January 1967), p54

[118] *Wight Report* issue 16, 'Island Railway Notes & News' (Winter 1971-72), p4

[119] See Appendix

[120] *Isle of Wight County Press*, 'Invincible Has a Bubbling Send of at Steam Rail Extravaganza' (31 August 1984), p11

[121] *Isle of Wight County Press*, 'BR Catching Up on Their Track Work' (19 April 1984), p13

[122] *Motive Power Monthly*, 'Rolling Stock Newsreel' (August 1988), p37

[123] *Rail*, 'Traction Talk' (November 1988), p58

[124] *Rail* (February 1989), p8

[125] *Motive Power Monthly*, 'Rolling Stock Newsreel' (November 1990), p44

[126] *Rail*, 'Uncertain Future for Island Line Class 03s' (14 August-27 August 1996), p14

[127] *Rail*, 'The "03" – The Humble Shunter That Took 28 Years to Die' (1 January-14 January 1997), p56

[128] R. C. Humphries, *Island Line* (2003), p55

[129] *The Railway Magazine*, 'Class 03 Returned to the Mainland for Front-line Use!' (August 1988), p7

[130] *Island Rail News* no 14, 'Ballast Train for Hire' (May-July 2002), p16

[131] *Isle of Wight County Press*, '"Spitfire" Arrives at Centre' (17 June 1972), p13

[132] T. E. Hastings (ed), *The Isle of Wight Steam Railway*, 4th Edition (enlarged) (1978), p31

[133] *Isle of Wight County Press*, 'Car Boot Sale, Auto Jumble and Boat Chandlery' (19 October 1984), p38

[134] *Rail*, 'Traction Talk' (January 1989), p38

Chapter Six

[135] *Motive Power Monthly* (May 1987), pp4-5

[136] *Rail Enthusiast*, 'Traction Talk' (May 1987), p48

[137] *Motive Power Monthly* (April 1987), p10

[138] *Isle of Wight County Press*, 'Railway Halt Suggested for Lake' (12 February 1966), p7

[139] See Appendix

[140] *Isle of Wight County Press*, 'Lake Protest Over Cash Towards New Rail Station' (12 December 1986), p1

[141] *Isle of Wight County Press*, 'New Station for Line "Has Wider Implications"' (28 November 1986), p3

[142] *Isle of Wight County Press*, '300 People a Day Using New Station' (17 July 1987), p41

[143] *Motive Power Monthly*, 'Station Developments' (August 1987), p11

[144] *Isle of Wight County Press*, '300 People a Day Using New Station' (17 July 1987), p41

[145] M. Brinton MIET, *A Technical Response to the Report: 'The Future of Island Line – Options Report'*, (March 2016)

[146] *Rail Enthusiast*, 'Departmental Developments' (October 1987), p40

[147] *Rail*, 'Traction Talk' (August 1988), p59

148 *Motive Power Monthly*, 'Rolling Stock Newsreel' (August 1988), p40
149 *Isle of Wight County Press,* '"New" Trains bought for IW Railway' (26 August 1988), p1
150 *Rail*, 'Traction Talk' (November 1988), p86
151 *Motive Power Monthly*, 'NSE Introduces Route Brandings' (August 1989), p8
152 *Rail*, 'Around the Regions' (January 1988), p28
153 *Wight Report* issue 2, 'By Tube from Ryde to Shanklin' (April 1968), p3
154 *The Guardian*, 'Diary' (18 January 1989), p23
155 *Rail*, 'Traction Talk' (February 1989), p55
156 *Rail*, 'Traction Talk' (23 March-5 April 1989), p56
157 *Motive Power Monthly* (June 1989), p5
158 *Isle of Wight County Press*, 'A Proud Day for the Island's Railways' (21 July 1989), p52
159 Ibid
160 *Wight Report* issue 82, 'IW Steam Railway News' (Winter 1988/89), pp161-162
161 *Rail*, 'Island Line "New" Stock in Service' (27 July-9 August 1989), p9
162 *Isle of Wight County Press*, 'Tourist Potential On Our Railway If Stock's Painted Southern Green' (21 April 1989), p10
163 *Motive Power Monthly*, 'Rolling Stock Newsreel' (August 1989), p40
164 *Isle of Wight County Press*, 'Rolling Stock Is Not So New…' (29 September 1989), p27
165 Dates taken from *Motive Power Monthly*, 'Rolling Stock Newsreel' (January 1990), p48
166 *Motive Power Monthly*, 'Rolling Stock Newsreel' (April 1990), p49
167 *Motive Power Monthly*, 'Rolling Stock Newsreel' (May 1990), p51
168 *Rail*, 'IoW Standard Stock Handover' (29 November-12 December 1990), p136
169 *Motive Power Monthly*, 'Rolling Stock Newsreel' (April 1990), p49
170 *Isle of Wight County Press*, 'Runaway Train Stopped by Scared Passengers' (18 January 1991), p3
171 *Isle of Wight County Press*, 'No Faults on Runaway Train' (1 February 1991), p3
172 *Rail*, 'Network (South) Rolling Stock Report' (27 May-9 June 1992), p53
173 *Motive Power Monthly*, 'Network SouthEast News' (November 1988), p8
174 *Rail*, 'Farewell to Classes 485/486' (2-15 November 1989), p45
175 *Motive Power Monthly*, 'More Island Line Changes' (January 1990), p37
176 *Rail*, 'Traction News' (31 May-13 June 1990), p55
177 *Network 2000* supplement p39, published with *Rail* (1-14 May 1991)
178 *The Railway Magazine*, 'Wight Update' (January 1994), p15
179 *Isle of Wight County Press*, 'Steam Boom Could See Railway Seek Further Expansion' (26 July 1991), p28
180 *Rail*, 'Potential Buyers for Isle of Wight Line' (19 October-1 November 1989), p5
181 *Rail*, 'Around the Regions' (23 March-5 April 1989), p21
182 *Rail*, 'Around the Regions' (1-14 November 1990), p23
183 *Rail*, 'Around the Regions' (2-15 September 1992), p21
184 *Model Rail* supplement 'Ventnor: A Model Re-opening' pp9-10, published with *Rail* (2-15 February 1994)
185 *Rail*, 'Island Line "New" Stock in Service' (27 July-9 August 1989), p9
186 *Rail*, 'Isle of Wight Stock to be Preserved' (18-31 October 1990), p11
187 *Motive Power Monthly*, 'Rolling Stock Newsreel' (June 1991), p49
188 *Motive Power Monthly*, 'Rolling Stock Newsreel' (July 1991), p48
189 B. Hardy, *Tube Trains on the Isle of Wight* (2003), p46
190 *Rail*, 'Island Line Loses Last 1925 Stock' (11-24 May 1994), p6
191 *Rail*, 'IOW Standard Stock Handover' (29 November-12 December 1990), p12
192 *Rail*, 'Cockfosters 1938' (5-18 February 1992), p7
193 Eastleigh Works has an unfortunate history of scrapping historic IOW vehicles once thought to have been set aside for preservation; the ex-IWR Beyer-Peacock 2-4-0T *Ryde* of 1864 was broken up there during the Second World War.

Chapter Seven

194 *Rail*, 'Potential Buyers for Isle of Wight Line' (19 October-1 November 1989), p5
195 *The Guardian*, 'Travel Agent's Offer to Run Island Line' (6 April 1963), p12
196 *Rail*, 'Island Line Bid' (19 August-1 September 1992), p18
197 *The Times*, 'How Not to Run a Railway' (6 February 1993), p14
198 *Rail*, 'Island View' (17-30 March 1993), p18
199 *The Guardian*, 'Rail Buy-out is on Wight Track, Says Island Group' (8 February 1993), p4
200 *Rail*, 'Island Line Bid' (19 August-1 September 1992), p18
201 *Rail*, 'Island View' (17-30 March 1993), p18

[202] *Rail*, 'Island View' (28 April-11 May 1993), p18
[203] *Rail*, 'Island Railway Study' (12-25 May 1993), p13
[204] *The Guardian*, 'Diary' (30 July 1993), p18
[205] *Rail*, 'Island View' (13-26 October 1993), p17
[206] *The Guardian*, 'Rail Sale Timetable Faces Further Delay' (31 January 1994), p5
[207] *The Guardian*, 'Rail Sell-Off Delayed for Another Year' (23 March 1994), p2
[208] *Rail*, 'Privatisation and the Island Line' (11-24 May 1994), p6
[209] *Rail*, 'Island Subsidy Continues' (20 July-2 August 1994), p16
[210] *Rail*, 'Steve Knight's Inside View on Privatisation' (17-30 January 1996), p16
[211] *Rail*, 'Around the Regions' (13-26 March 1996), p19
[212] *Rail*, 'Confusion Over Island Line Bid' (3-16 July 1996), p63
[213] *Rail*, 'Privatisation' (17-30 July 1996), p28
[214] *Rail*, 'Privatisation' (28 August-10 September 1996), p44
[215] *Rail*, 'Privatisation' (23 October–5 November 1996), p29
[216] *Rail*, 'Ventnor Study Comes Nearer' (20 July-2 August 1994), p17
[217] *Rail*, 'Go-ahead Given for Ventnor Study' (12-25 October 1994), p6
[218] *Rail*, 'Ventnor Extension Endorsed' (7-20 December 1994), p7
[219] *Rail*, 'Isle of Wight's Ventnor Extension Plans' (31 January-13 February 1996), p8
[220] *Isle of Wight County Press*, 'Expert Study Backs Rail Link to Ventnor' (26 January 1996), p1
[221] Ibid
[222] *Isle of Wight County Press*, 'Railway Scheme Runs Into Row Over Village Voice' (19 April 1996), p6
[223] *Isle of Wight County Press*, 'Views of Ordinary Wroxall Residents Not Being Heard' (10 May 1996), p10
[224] *Isle of Wight County Press*, 'Funding Blow for Ventnor Rail Link' (7 February 1997), p1
[225] *The Times*, 'The Lady's Got a Ticket to Ryde' (28 August 1999), p19
[226] *Rail*, 'Island View' (13-26 October 1993), p17
[227] *Rail*, 'Around the Regions' (11-24 September 1996), p20
[228] *The Times*, 'Stagecoach Line Rallies' (1 December 1997), p49
[229] *The Times*, 'Never Mind That Your Train is Late Again, Think of the Fat Profits' (4 May 1998), p44
[230] *The Times*, 'The Lady's Got a Ticket to Ryde' (28 August 1999), p19
[231] The Isle of Wight is one of the richest dinosaur fossil-hunting grounds in Europe, something that the tourist industry has been keen to capitalise on ever since the Island's first fibreglass dinosaurs were airlifted into Blackgang Chine in 1972.
[232] *Isle of Wight County Press*, 'Rail Passengers Now Riding With Dinosaurs' (24 March 2000), p1
[233] *Isle of Wight County Press*, 'Dinosaur Livery Wrong For IslandLine' (14 April 2000), p17
[234] *Island Rail News*, '007 – Licensed to Thrill' (May-July 2003), p17
[235] Strategic Rail Authority/GIBB Transport Consulting, *Island Line Replacement Review Executive Summary* (2001)

Chapter Eight

[236] *Isle of Wight County Press*, 'In For a Penny' (30 March 2007), p4
[237] *Isle of Wight County Press*, 'New Lease of Life for Ryde Trains' (23 March 2007), p13
[238] *Isle of Wight County Press*, '£200,000 Boost for Stations' (7 September 2007), p20
[239] *Isle of Wight County Press*, 'Town Considers List of Improvements' (3 October 2003), p7
[240] *Isle of Wight County Press*, 'Buzzing Brading Takes the Biscuit' (30 December 2005), p12
[241] *Isle of Wight County Press*, 'Loving Care Adds New Lease of Life' (28 April 2006), p12
[242] *Isle of Wight County Press*, 'All Aboard for Stations' Clean Up' (27 June 2008), p33
[243] Strategic Rail Authority/GIBB Transport Consulting, *Island Line Replacement Review Executive Summary* (2001), p7
[244] *Isle of Wight County Press*, 'Massive Cash Aid Spells Bright Future for Ryde' (1 September 2000), p21
[245] *Isle of Wight County Press*, 'Public Back Interchange Project' (15 June 2001), p39
[246] *Isle of Wight County Press*, 'Island's Green Landscape Inspires Interchange's Leafy Look' (8 April 2005), p3
[247] *The Railway Magazine*, 'Transformation Planned for Ryde Esplanade' (May 2006), p82
[248] *Isle of Wight County Press*, 'Ryde Interchange May Be Delayed Due to Contracts' (7 December 2007), p8
[249] *Isle of Wight County Press*, 'Delayed Transport Site Gets a Tidy-Up' (7 March 2008), p4
[250] *Isle of Wight County Press*, 'Gateway Closes' (9 October 2009), p1
[251] *Isle of Wight County Press*, 'Time to Spend on Ryde' (5 February 2010), p17
[252] *Isle of Wight County Press*, 'IW Rail Control Signalled' (22 August 2014), p3
[253] *Isle of Wight County Press*, 'Save Our Trains' (17 July 2015), p1
[254] *Isle of Wight County Press*, 'IW Rail Control Signalled' (22 August 2014), p3
[255] *Isle of Wight County Press*, 'Steam Return "Pure Fantasy"' (28 November 2014), p26
[256] *Isle of Wight County Press*, 'Steaming Back into Ryde?' (19 December 2014), p1

257 *Isle of Wight County Press*, 'Steam Railway Keen to Extend to Ryde' (9 January 2015), p45

258 *Island Rail News*, 'A Return to Ryde St John's Road Please!' (November-January 2003/04), p22

259 *Isle of Wight County Press*, 'Steam Railway Keen to Extend to Ryde' (9 January 2015), p45

260 *Isle of Wight County Press*, 'Revamp of Island Line Supported by Minister' (20 February 2015), p22

261 *Isle of Wight County Press*, 'Focus on Future of Island Line' (3 July 2015), p4

262 *Isle of Wight County Press*, '"Bombshell" News for Island Line' (10 July 2015), p9

263 *Isle of Wight County Press*, 'Keep Our Railway Part of Regional Franchise' (10 July 2015), p51

264 *Isle of Wight County Press*, 'Future of IW Rail Services Comes Under Scrutiny' (17 July 2015), p43

265 *Isle of Wight County Press*, 'Council Plans to Keep Rail Service on Right Track' (21 July 2000), p3

266 *Isle of Wight County Press*, 'Blurred Lines' (31 July 2015), p14

267 *Isle of Wight County Press*, 'Steam Railway Should Be Given a Chance' (31 July 2015), p45

268 *Isle of Wight County Press*, 'Steam Railway Won't Run It' (31 July 2015), p14

269 *Isle of Wight County Press*, 'Now MP Says Island Line Should Remain in Franchise' (4 September 2015), p4

270 *Isle of Wight County Press*, 'The Future of IW Railways' (11 September 2015), p47

271 *Isle of Wight County Press*, 'Island MP Determined to Push Ahead with Transport Task Force (18 September 2015), p13

272 *Isle of Wight County Press*, 'Transport Expert to Search for Island Line Solutions' (16 October 2015), p7

273 *Isle of Wight County Press*, 'New Concerns Over Island Line Adviser' (23 October 2015), p17

274 *Isle of Wight County Press*, 'Row Over Cancelled Interview with Journalist' (23 October 2015), p17

275 *The Railway Magazine*, 'Wight Steam to Return to Ryde?' (January 2015), p10

276 *The Railway Magazine*, 'Controversy Raging Over Proposals for Island Line' (November 2015), p8

277 *The Railway Magazine*, 'Island Line Future Part of SWT Franchise Consultation' (December 2015), p9

278 *Isle of Wight County Press*, 'Government Officials Say No Decision Yet on Island Line Franchise Status' (18 December 2015), p12

279 *Isle of Wight County Press*, '"Train report was worth the money"' (11 December 2015), p8

280 C. Garnett, *The future of Island Line - Options Report* (January 2016)

281 *Isle of Wight County Press*, 'Steam Railway Boss Backs Trams Idea' (19 February 2016), p21

282 *Isle of Wight County Press*, 'MP Says We Must Look for Alternatives' (12 February 2016), p59

283 *Isle of Wight County Press*, 'Council Still Wants Rail Line in the Franchise' (12 February 2016), p59

284 M. Brinton MIET, *A Technical Response to the Report: 'The Future of Island Line – Options Report'* (March 2016)

285 *Isle of Wight County Press*, 'Council Wants Island Line To Stay in Franchise' (18 March 2016), p12

286 *Isle of Wight County Press*, 'Island Line Row May Go to Court' (5 August 2016), p10

287 *Isle of Wight County Press*, 'Joy Over Island Line Climb Down' (12 August 2016), p8

288 *Rail*, 'DfT Change of Heart Over "Sustainable" Island Line' (31 August-13 September 2016), p23

289 South Western Railway, *Developing a More Sustainable Future for Island Line* (2017)

290 *Isle of Wight County Press*, 'Group Set Up To Look at IW's Transport Problems' (22 July 2016), p15

291 *The Railway Magazine*, 'Talks Begin on Future of Island Line Operations' (January 2018), p66

292 *The Railway Magazine*, 'Island Line Deserves Better' (December 2015), p32

293 *Rail*, 'D-Train attracts American Interest … As Vivarail Talks to UK Companies' (4-17 July 2018), p16

294 *Modern Railways*, 'Vivarail Delivers First Class 230' (October 2018), p76

295 *The Railway Magazine*, 'DfT Decision on Island Line Future Deferred for Three Months' (February 2019), p6

296 *Isle of Wight County Press*, 'The Future of IW Railways' (11 September 2015), p47

297 *Isle of Wight County Press*, 'Rail Group Fears for Trains on Pier' (15 July 2016), p1

298 Letter from Robert Seely MBE MP to Jo Johnson MP, *Island Line Priced Option,* 5 November 2018

299 *Isle of Wight County Press*, 'Good News for Island Line Passengers – Government Pledges to Maintain Ryde Pier Railway Line' (4 January 2018), www.countypress.co.uk/news/17332877.article

300 *Steam Railway*, 'Isle of Wight Steam Could Return to Ryde in 2021' (1-28 March 2019), p10

301 *Isle of Wight County Press*, '"Modern" Steam Train Puffs to the Rescue' (15 July 2016), p9

302 Isle of Wight Steam Railway, *Strategic Vision* (June 2009, revised 2017), p14

Bibliography

Developing a More Sustainable Future for Island Line (South Western Railway, 2017)

The Future of Island Line – Options Report by C. Garnett (20 January 2016)

The Great Isle of Wight Train Robbery by R. E. Burroughs (Railway Invigoration Society, 1968)

Island Line by R. C. Humphries (Coach House Publications, 2003)

Island Line Replacement Review Executive Summary (Strategic Rail Authority/GIBB Transport Consulting, September 2001)

Island Line – Technical Advisory by W. Lowe & H. Chaplain (Atkins, 16 September 2015)

Island Rail News, various issues

The Isle of Wight County Press, various issues

The Isle of Wight Railway: 40 Years of Preservation by D. Walker & T. Hastings (Nostalgia Road Publications, 2006)

The Isle of Wight Railway Stock Book by R. Silsbury (Isle of Wight Railway Co. Ltd, 1994)

The Isle of Wight Railways from 1923 Onwards by R. J. Maycock & R. Silsbury (Oakwood Press, 2006)

The Isle of Wight Steam Railway by T. E. Hastings (ed) (Isle of Wight Railway Co. Ltd, 4th edition, 1978)

Isle of Wight Steam Railway: Strategic Vision (Isle of Wight Railway Co. Ltd, June 2009, revised 2017)

Modern Railways, Vol. 75 No. 841, October 2018

Modern Tramway and Light Rail Transit, Vol. 50 No. 594, June 1987

Motive Power Monthly, various issues

The Piers, Tramways and Railways at Ryde by R. J. Maycock & R. Silsbury (Oakwood Press, 2005)

Rail (formerly *Rail Enthusiast*), various issues

The Railway Magazine, various issues

The Railways and Tramways of Ryde by A. Blackburn & J. Mackett (Town & Country Press, 1971)

The Reshaping of British Railways Part I: Report (HMSO, 1963)

Steam Railway, No. 490, 1-28 March 2019

A Technical Response to the Report: "The Future of Island Line – Options Report" by M. Brinton MIET (March 2016)

Tube Trains on the Isle of Wight by B. Hardy (Capital Transport, 2003)

Wight Report, various issues

Online resources

Isle of Wight Community Rail Partnership: www.isleofwightcrp.co.uk

Isle of Wight County Press Archive: http://archive.iwcp.co.uk

Isle of Wight Steam Railway: www.iwsteamrailway.co.uk

Keep Island Line in Franchise (KILF) Facebook group: www.facebook.com/groups/kilfcampaign

On the Wight: www.onthewight.com

ProQuest Historical Newspapers: www.proquest.com/products-services/pq-hist-news.html

The Railway Magazine Digital Archive: www.railwaymagazine.co.uk/archive

The Times Digital Archive: www.gale.com/intl/c/the-times-digital-archive

Index

1938 Stock (conversion).............................74-77, 80-82

1938 Stock (dinosaur livery)...................95-98, 101-103

1938 Stock (entry into service)..............................76-82

1938 Stock (Network SouthEast livery).......... 76, 80, 82, 93, 98

1938 Stock (numbering and formations)..............74-77, 81-82, 93, 98, 122-123

1938 Stock (red livery) 97-98, 101-103

1938 Stock (replacement) 89, 95, 98, 110, 115-117, 119-120, 122-123

1938 Stock (ride quality) 82, 100, 116

1938 Stock (suitability for Isle of Wight).....51-52, 55, 74

1938 Stock (withdrawals and disposal).........93, 122-123

Acton 17, 48, 86, 98

Atkins Report.. 114

Bacon, Cllr Jonathan 111-112, 115-116

Beeching Report 7-10, 28

Bennie Airspeed Railway 8

Brading......................12, 25, 44-45, 47, 52, 66, 73-74, 79-80, 89, 93, 100, 103-105, 111, 115, 119-120, 122

Branding, see Signage and branding

Brinton, Mark 116

Calbourne............................... 17, 21, 36, 62, 64, 82, 85

Class 03...64-68, 85

Class 05...21, 26, 60-64, 68

Class 230, see Vivarail

Class 483, see 1938 Stock

Class 485 (4-VEC), see Standard Stock

Class 486 (3-TIS), see Standard Stock

Class 503.....................52-56, 64, 73-74, 120, Appendix

Costed Option 117, 119, 120-121

Cowes 8-10, 12, 14-16, 28, 43-44

D Stock...56, 119-120

Department for Transport (DfT) 110-122

Diesel shunters, see Class 03, Class 05

Dinosaur livery, see 1938 Stock (dinosaur livery)

Eastleigh 8, 60, 64, 66, 75, 76, 80-81, 86

Electrification 9, 15-16, 21, 26, 29, 44, 62, 64, 73, 100, 110, 116

End of steam 15, 21

Eversholt Leasing/HSBC Rail 93, 101, 103

First Group/MTR..116-117

Fratton..60, 76, 80-81, 84-85

Garnett, Christopher.................................114-117, 119

Green, Chris 73, 77, 80, 82, 84-85, 88

Havenstreet, see Isle of Wight Steam Railway

Hovercraft.. 14, 110, 115, 119

HSBC Rail, see Eversholt Leasing

Infrastructure lease 90, 110, 119-122

Island Line (brand)..........74-75, 80, 90, 93, 95, 101, 117

Island Line (separate franchise).......................67, 89-101

Island Vintage Transport Group (IVTG)........................ 36

Isle of Wight Council (unitary authority) 100, 107-117

Isle of Wight County Council 7-9, 12, 28-29, 43-45, 56, 73, 88-89, 91-92, 100

Isle of Wight Steam Railway (IWSR)................. 8, 17, 36, 42, 62, 64, 66-68, 73-74, 79-80, 82, 85, 89-91, 103, 105, 107, 110-112, 114-117, 119-120, 122-123

Keep Island Line in Franchise (KILF)............112, 114-117, 121-122

Lake 55, 73, 90, 100, 107

Landguard Manor Road Bridge 47, 91

Light Rail............. 9, 44, 89, 91, 100, 111, 115-116, 119

Loading gauge....................8, 11, 15, 21, 28, 52-53, 60, 64, 89, 100, 115-116, 119-120

London Transport Museum 85-86, 123

London Underground 11, 16-17, 26, 29, 48, 51-52, 56, 74-75, 85-86, 97-98, 101-103, 120, 123

Marples, Ernest.. 12-13

Medina Wharf 10, 15

Moquette 17, 56, 98

Network SouthEast 66-67, 70-84, 88- 91, 93, 98

Newport 7, 10, 12, 15, 21, 36, 43-44, 46-47

Nuclear Fred, see Class 05

Platform heights 11, 17, 24, 53, 82, 116, 120

Priced Option, *see* Costed Option

Privatisation 84, 88-91

Pugh, David 111-112, 115, 122

Rink Road Bridge 64, 120

Runaway train.. 81

Ryde Depot................ 17, 48, 53, 55-56, 59, 62, 64, 66, 70, 74, 76-77, 82, 84-85, 93, 98, 101, 116

Ryde Esplanade....................7, 10-12, 21, 24-25, 34-37, 45-47, 53-55, 74, 80, 89-90, 100, 107-110, 115-116, 121

Ryde Gateway/Ryde Interchange....................... 107-110

Ryde Pier 7, 9-12, 15-16, 21, 24-26, 28, 30-42, 44-46, 51, 53-55, 59, 62-64, 73-74, 80, 85, 89, 93, 100, 110, 114-115, 121-122

Ryde Pier Head 7, 9-12, 14-16, 24-26, 30-41, 45-47, 53, 55-56, 60, 64, 73, 77-80, 89, 93, 100, 110, 115

Ryde Pier Shuttle.................... 34, 45-46, 55, 80, 93, 100

Ryde Pier Tram 10, 30-42, 45

Ryde Rail.. 58-59, 71, 75

Ryde St John's Road 7, 11-12, 16, 21, 25, 30, 34, 44-47, 53, 64, 66, 73, 80, 82, 85, 89, 93, 100, 107, 110-111, 115-116, 119-120, 122

Ryde Tunnel 11, 15, 21, 26, 46, 52-53, 60, 64, 89, 100, 110, 115-117, 119-120

Ryde Works, *see* Ryde Depot

Sadler-Vectrail 36, 43-44, 68

Sandown 1, 9-10, 21, 25-26, 28, 34, 44, 46-47, 60, 62, 66, 73-74, 77, 81, 84-85, 89, 100, 111, 120

Seely MP, Bob 117, 121

Shanklin..........................9-10, 12-16, 21, 25-29, 34, 36, 44-45, 47, 73, 81, 84, 89, 91, 100, 105

Signage and branding.............. 17, 25, 32, 56-59, 70-71, 74-75, 80, 90, 93, 95-98, 101-103, 105, 117

Signal boxes.................... 25, 45-47, 73, 79-80, 105, 110

Smallbrook Junction............21, 25, 43-44, 66-67, 73-74, 79-80, 82, 89-90, 98, 105, 107, 111, 115-116, 122-123

South West Trains (SWT) 90-91, 93, 101, 105, 110-111, 114-116

South Western franchise 101, 110-119, 121-122

South Western Railway (SWR) 117-122

Southern Railway 15-16, 25, 30, 56, 62, 73, 105

Southern Region 8-9, 15-16, 28-29, 32, 45-46, 71, 73

Southern Vectis.. 10, 88-91, 115

Stagecoach Group 90-91, 93-95, 100-101, 111-112, 116-117, 122

Standard Stock (Control Trailers) 16-17, 58, 71-73, 84-86

Standard Stock (conversion and arrival) 11, 15-17, 26, 48

Standard Stock (Driving Motors)................. 16-17, 48-50, 55-56, 58, 70-71, 75, 77, 85-86

Standard Stock (entry into service) 26-28

Standard Stock (liveries) 16-17, 56-58, 70-71

Standard Stock (numbering and set formations).... 16-17, 26, 48, 50, 56, 58, 70, 84

Standard Stock (preservation)........................... 81, 84-86

Standard Stock (replacement)..........43-44, 51-56, 74-79, 80-82, 84-85

Standard Stock (withdrawals and disposal)............ 48-50, 76-77, 81, 84-87

Stations 7, 15, 17, 24-25, 44, 46-47, 55, 70, 73, 75, 77-80, 82, 89, 93, 97, 100, 107, 114, 117, 120-121

Strategic Rail Authority (SRA) 100, 107

T69 trams 115-116, 119

TIS, *see* Standard Stock

Transport for London (TfL), *see* London
    Underground

Transport Users' Consultative Committee
    (TUCC) 12-14

Turner MP, Andrew 110-112, 114-115, 117

VEC, *see* Standard Stock

Vectrail, *see* Sadler-Vectrail

Ventnor 7-12, 14-15, 28-29, 44,
    47, 53, 84, 89, 91-92

Ventnor Railway Association (VRA)............... 84, 89,
    91-92, 100

Vertical franchise................................... 89, 91, 122

Vivarail.. 119-120

Wight Locomotive Society (WLS)....... 21, 29, 36-37,
    44, 62

Wightlink............................. 41, 68, 82, 88-90, 100

Woodnutt MP, Ald. Mark 7, 9-10, 13-14, 28, 36

Wroxall 15, 29, 91-92

By the same author

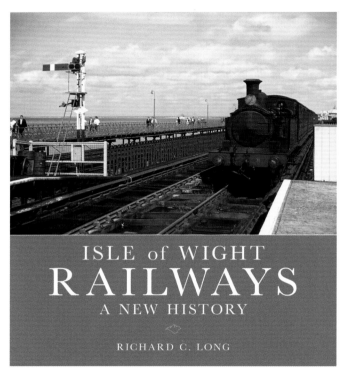

ISLE of WIGHT
RAILWAYS
A NEW HISTORY

RICHARD C. LONG

Isle of Wight Railways: A New History

Richard C Long

Although the Isle of Wight railway network reached an extent of only 55 miles, the special character of its trains and routes is fondly remembered by many.

In *Isle of Wight Railways: A New History*, detailed new research presents a fresh look at the history and development of the railways on the island.

Richard C Long has undertaken comprehensive research to present interesting findings on the development of the railway's network, all illustrated with a fantastic selection of colour photographs, many of which have never been published before,

The Isle of Wight railways are always popular with railway aficionados, and this book takes a fresh look at their history and development, making it a must have for modellers and enthusiasts alike.

ISBN: 9780711038165
Hardback, 96 pages, £20